EMERGENCY FIRST AID

Safety Oriented

Fourth Edition 1990

St. John Ambulance
312 Laurier Avenue East
Ottawa, Canada K1N 6P6

First Edition	–	*1977*
Second Edition	–	*1984*
Third Edition	–	*1988*
Fourth Edition	–	*1990*
First Impression (1990)	–	*120,000*

Canadian Cataloguing in Publication Data

Main entry under title:
    Emergency first aid: safety oriented

Fourth Edition 1990

Issued also in French under title: Secourisme
    d'urgence : orienté vers la sécurité.
ISBN 0-929006-12-7
(ISBN: 0-919434-80-0. 3ʳᵈ edition, 1988)

1. First aid in illness and injury -- Handbooks,
manuals, etc.   I. St. John Ambulance.

RC87.E44 1990   616.02'52   C90-090286-8

This publication has been adopted by the Canadian
Forces and has been assigned NDID number:
A-MD-101-002/PT-001.

Printed in Canada   Stock number: 3410

CONTENTS

FOREWORD TO THE SECOND EDITION

The end of W.W. II heralded the beginning of the Atomic Age, and within a few years nuclear weapons were widespread and a constant threat to the human race. If the bombs fly, death and injuries will be counted by the millions, swamping existing medical facilities and trained personnel. Evacuation and treatment of casualties must be simplified, streamlined and accelerated. To achieve significant benefits in such desperate circumstances, there must be large numbers of First Aiders to concentrate their attention on the survivors.

In 1951, Civil Defence authorities in the Department of National Health and Welfare designated St. John Ambulance (Priory of Canada) as the official organization responsible for teaching first aid for Civil Defence. A Committee was appointed by the Priory to produce a new Textbook of First Aid. It was published under the title "Fundamentals of First Aid, 1955." The new book seemed to meet the need rather well and was widely acclaimed.

"Fundamentals" proved to be an excellent outline of basic first aid applicable to all types of civilian or military injuries. In addition, a small section on "Special Weapons" dealt briefly with nuclear, biological and chemical weapons, including nerve gas and blister gas. The concept was then established that routine first aid techniques could be applied to injuries from the various special weapons just as effectively as they are used to care for the accidental injuries and sudden illnesses which we see from day to day.

A new concept has been introduced into first aid in recent years; namely, to integrate teaching of accident prevention along with techniques for first aid. Managers and workers must understand that it is much more efficient to prevent accidents and injuries than to treat the resulting illness, pain and disability, which are the costs of carelessness.

Programmes of accident prevention must be introduced and emphasized at every opportunity, particularly when real-life incidents can be used as examples of injuries which might, with care, have been avoided.

R.A. Mustard, C.St.J, M.D., F.R.C.S.(C).
January, 1984

PREFACE TO THE THIRD EDITION

The third edition of Emergency First Aid Safety Oriented was prepared, primarily, to reflect those changes in artificial respiration and first aid for choking adopted by the Canadian Heart Foundation (Heart and Stroke Foundation of Canada). In its continuing efforts to keep first aid material current, St. John Ambulance has also included other changes recommended by the National Medical Advisory Committee.

Safety content has been increased, particularly in the area of the handling of hazardous materials in the workplace. This reflects the growing concerns in occupational health and safety resulting from increased use of controlled products. These concerns are addressed more fully in the Workplace Hazardous Products Information System (WHMIS).

The manual, along with the video series St. John Ambulance Presents and the Student Workbook, continues to support training at the Emergency First Aid Certificate level. However, it is also an excellent reference manual for the workplace and the home, and should be in all first aid kits.

J.J. Benoit,
Brigadier General
OStJ, CD, QHP, BA, MD, CRCPC, CSPQ
Chief Medical Officer — St. John Ambulance
November 1988

Note: *This fourth edition of Emergency First Aid Safety Oriented was prepared as a result of changes in the medical recommendations for certain first aid procedures. Consequently, the first aid for poisonings, eye injuries, snake and insect bites and a variety of other medical emergencies has been completely updated and included in this fourth edition.*

R.L. Rowlatt
National Director of Training — St. John Ambulance
August 1990

ACKNOWLEDGEMENTS

St. John Ambulance, the Priory of Canada, records grateful acknowledgement to those who granted permission to use certain material or otherwise contributed to the production of this manual, in particular the Industrial Accident Prevention Association of Ontario and the Heart and Stroke Foundation of Canada.

EDITORIAL BOARD — SECOND EDITION

1

PRINCIPLES AND PRACTICES OF SAFETY ORIENTED FIRST AID

PRINCIPLES OF SAFETY

There are risks in most activities of daily living, but these risks can be eliminated or considerably reduced if you know what they are and if you take appropriate actions and safeguards. As a First Aider, you will know the terrible consequences of injury. This will motivate you to recognize hazards and to apply the principles of safety to avoid such injuries.

Applying the principles of safety means that you will:

- **assess risks** and report accident potentials. Learn the risks of working with hazardous materials as detailed on product labels and in the *Workplace Hazardous Materials Information System (WHMIS)*. You should acquaint yourself also with the *Dangerous Goods Placards and Labels* used to identify hazardous materials during transportation.

- **plan the activity** so that the job can be performed safely and so that dangerous situations can be controlled as they arise. Take the precautions recommended on label instructions and *Material Safety Data Sheets (MSDS)*.

- **train for the job** so that you can work safely with equipment and materials, recognize unsafe conditions and take appropriate steps to eliminate the accident potential.

- **use personal protective equipment** recommended in job training and in material safety data sheets, such as gloves, aprons, boots, clothing, goggles, face shields, respirators, safety harnesses, etc.

- **make a personal commitment to safety** at home, in leisure activities, and in the workplace, for others as well as yourself. Be constantly aware of accident potentials and eliminate or report such hazards.

Learn to recognize hazardous product symbols on consumer products in the home. Take the precautions and follow the first aid directions indicated on container labels.

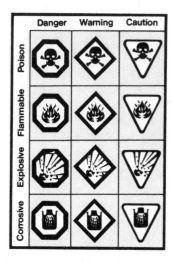

Fig. 1-1. Hazardous products symbols.

Hazardous products in the workplace display one of the following WHMIS symbols that include warnings on flammability, reactivity, and health risk, and indicate the personal protection required. An associated MSDS includes first aid instructions in the event of an accident. Familiarize yourself with these instructions.

If you come upon the scene of a transportation accident involving any suspected dangerous chemicals or materials, look for *Dangerous Goods Placards* on the vehicle or *Dangerous Goods Labels* on containers. If assistance is needed in handling these materials, contact the Canadian Transport Emergency Centre (CANUTEC) by phoning area code (6l3) 996-6666 collect.

Class	Symbol	Division
A		**COMPRESSED GAS**
B		**FLAMMABLE AND COMBUSTIBLE MATERIAL**
C		**OXIDIZING MATERIAL**
D		**POISONOUS AND INFECTIOUS MATERIALS**
D-1		Materials causing immediate and serious toxic effect.
D-2		Material causing other toxic effects.
D-3		Biohazardous infectious material.
E		**CORROSIVE MATERIAL**
F		**DANGEROUS REACTIVE MATERIAL**

Extracted from *Canada Gazette*, Part II, Vol. 122, No. 2, January 20, 1988

Fig. 1-2. Workplace hazardous materials symbols.

SAFETY OF THE FIRST AIDER AND CASUALTY

First aid situations often pose risks because they demand quick action under dangerous conditions. Therefore, the primary duty of a First Aider is to protect himself and by-standers from harm and to protect the casualty from further injuries. To do this, be aware of the hazards in any accident situation. These are:

- the forces that caused the initial injury, such as machines, electrical energy, fire, chemicals, environmental conditions, etc.;

- other conditions that may cause further injury, such as spilled fuel, unsafe buildings, motor traffic, etc.;

- rescue or first aid procedures that may cause you injury or further injury to the casualty, for example, extrication, lifting, carrying, etc.

MEDICAL AID

Medical aid is the professional treatment given by or under the direction of a doctor at a medical facility or on the way to such a facility.

FIRST AID

First aid is the emergency care given to an injured or suddenly ill person, using readily available materials. First aid may be given while awaiting the arrival of medical aid or in preparation for transportation to medical aid.

Objectives of First Aid

The objectives of first aid are to:

- preserve life;

- prevent the injury or illness from becoming worse; and

- promote recovery.

Priorities in First Aid

First aid should be given for life-threatening conditions in the following priorities:

- stopped breathing;

- severe bleeding; and

- unconsciousness.

ACCIDENT SCENE MANAGEMENT

How you manage an accident scene will depend on how well you have prepared yourself. If you have learned the Priority Action Approach (PAA) and have confidence in your first aid skills, you should be able to take control of an accident situation and see to it that the casualty receives the best possible first aid safely and that he is handed over to medical aid without delay. Accident scene management can be divided into two parts:

- PAA; and

- continuing first aid.

PRIORITY ACTION APPROACH

Priority action approach is the sequence of actions you should take on arrival at the scene of an accident or sudden illness to ensure that life-saving first aid is given safely. You may have to change the order of the following steps slightly to meet changing circumstances, but generally they should be performed in the following sequence:

1. Take charge of the situation.

2. Call to attract the attention of bystanders to assist you.

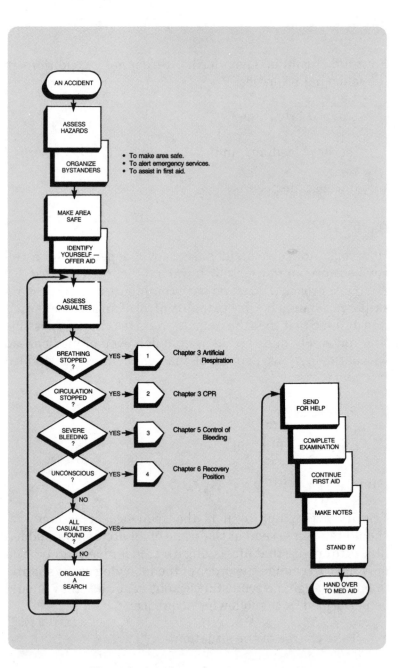

Fig. 1-3. Accident scene management.

3.   Assess hazards — from the original cause of the accident as well as secondary causes.

4.   Make the area safe for yourself and others.

5.   Identify yourself as a First Aider and offer to help.

6.   Quickly assess the casualty for life-threatening conditions.

7.   Give first aid for life-threatening conditions.

8.   Send someone to call for help — police, ambulance, etc.

CONTINUING FIRST AID

When the casualty's life is no longer in danger and while awaiting the arrival of medical aid, continue giving first aid by performing a **secondary examination** if indicated and giving whatever first aid is needed.

MAKE THE AREA SAFE

Look quickly for anything that may cause harm to yourself or to the casualty, and take all precautions to prevent injury before starting first aid. In particular, do the following:

- turn off vehicle ignition, switch off motors and shut down machines.

- switch off electric power, or use a long dry stick or other nonconductive material to remove live housewires from a casualty. Do not attempt to remove high tension electric wires until a power company official gives permission. *The electrical energy from high tension wires discharging into the ground can kill.* If there is no immediate danger, tell the casualty not to move and to stay calm. Advise occupants to remain in a car that is in contact with high voltage electric wires unless there are other immediate dangers. The rubber tires on the car act as insulators, and the occupants are safe as long as they do not touch the ground and a metal part of the car at the same time. If other dangers force them to leave, instruct them to jump clear so that they will not complete a circuit by touching the car and the ground at the same time. Caution them not to fall forward on their hands nor to land with their feet apart. This may cause an electric current to pass through the body. Advise them to shuffle with the feet together *(not to run or walk)* until they are a safe distance from the car. Do not attempt rescues from such vehicles until power company officials have declared it safe to do so.

- prevent chemical spills from spreading, and take precautions to prevent fire and explosions if this can be done safely.

- redirect traffic around a road accident when a casualty is exposed to further injury from moving vehicles.

If the casualty is exposed to further injury and the rescue does not pose a grave danger, move him to safety before starting first aid. Do not move a casualty unless it is absolutely necessary for his safety, to give him life-saving first aid or to get him to medical aid *(see chap. 14 - Rescue and Transportation)*.

CASUALTY ASSESSMENT

History, Signs and Symptoms

The information needed to assess a casualty's injury or illness is grouped under three headings: history, signs and symptoms. In first aid, these terms are defined as follows:

- **history** — the events leading to the accident, evidence of violence, the circumstances of an injury or a record of previous illness *(see chap. 6 - Unconsciousness)*.

- **signs** — those conditions you can see or observe that indicate disease or injury. Three of these, body temperature, pulse and breathing, are called **vital signs** because they may indicate the presence or absence of life. Other signs, which will help you to recognize specific injuries and illnesses, are described in later chapters.

- **symptoms** — the sensations that a person feels, usually discomfort due to heat, cold, pain, nausea and other sensations that are not normal. The absence of feeling or numbness is also a symptom.

Be on the alert, when giving first aid, for information that may tell you what happened *(history)*; for changes in temperature, pulse and breathing *(vital signs)* and for the casualty's complaints *(symptoms)*. Learn to recognize and interpret these so that correct first aid can be given.

Primary Examination

Give the casualty a quick primary examination for life-threatening conditions and give first aid to:

- **restore breathing**. Open the airway, give artificial respiration *(see chap. 3 - Artificial Respiration)*.

- **stop severe bleeding.** Apply direct pressure, elevate the injured limb and put the casualty at rest *(see chap.5 - Wounds and Bleeding)*.

- **protect the unconscious casualty**. Place him in the recovery position to prevent the tongue falling to the back of the throat and affecting breathing *(see chap.3- Artificial Respiration and chap. 6 - Unconsciousness).*

Identify and give first aid for all life-threatening conditions in all casualties before conducting a secondary examination. For any casualty with a suspected head or neck injury, steady and support the head and neck before assessing responsiveness. Once first aid for life-threatening conditions has been given, apply a cervical collar.

Secondary Examination

When all immediate threats to life have been removed, carry out a secondary examination. If the casualty is conscious, be guided by his complaints of pain or numbness, and examine those areas first, but do not examine for unlikely injuries. A complete body examination may be necessary, particularly if the person is unconscious. Make such an examination systematically, starting at the head and working all the way down the body to the extremities. The First Aider should search for medical information (eg: Medic-Alert device) that may give information about the person's condition. Unless the casualty is in immediate danger, do not reposition him for the purpose of conducting this examination:

- **temperature** — feel the forehead and the back of the neck to see if the skin temperature is much warmer or cooler than that of your hand.

- **pulse** — check the pulse, noting its rate, strength and rhythm. *(see chap. 2 - The Body and Its Functions).*

- **breathing** — note its rate, rhythm and depth and smell the breath for distinctive odours of chemicals or acetone *(see chap. 12 - Poisons and chap. 13 -Medical Conditions).*

- **eyes** — note if pupils are fully dilated, constricted, or of unequal size, and then check for reaction to light *(see chap. 13 - Medical Conditions)*.

- **ears and nose** — look for blood and other fluid discharge that may indicate skull injuries *(see chap. 8 - Injuries to Bones and Joints)*.

- **mouth** — check the mouth for fluids or vomitus that might affect breathing.

- **skin** — note the colour, the amount of perspiration and the temperature *(see chap. 7 - Shock and chap. 13 - Medical Conditions)*.

- **skull** — check for bruises, bumps or bleeding that may indicate head injuries *(see chap. 8 - Injuries to Bones and Joints)*.

- **neck** — check the neck gently. If there is pain, or deformity, suspect a fracture of the spine at the neck *(see chap. 8 - Injuries to Bones and Joints)*.

- **spine** — feel along the centre line of the back for irregularities. If there is bleeding *(you feel an area that is warm and wet)* or if there is tenderness and pain, suspect a fracture of the spine *(see chap. 8 - Injuries to Bones and Joints)*.

- **chest area** — look for wounds and note any unnatural movement of the chest. Gently feel the ribs with the fingertips for irregularities or, if the casualty is conscious, ask him to take a deep breath and cough. Pain and tenderness indicate a possible fracture of the ribs or sternum *(see chap. 8 - Injuries to Bones and Joints)*.

- **abdominal area** — look for wounds and bleeding and ask the casualty to pull in and push out the abdomen.

Suspect internal injuries if this causes pain *(see chap. 5 - Wounds and Bleeding)*.

- **pelvic area** — gently feel on either side of the hips for signs of tenderness or irregularities that might indicate a fracture of the pelvis or dislocation of the hip *(see chap. 8 - Injuries to Bones and Joints)*.

- **lower and upper limbs** — check the limbs for irregularities in the long bones or joints. To assess for nerve injury and loss of power, ask the casualty if he has feeling in the fingers and toes and if he can move the limbs *(see chap. 8 - Injuries to Bones and Joints)*.

FOLLOW -UP CARE

Give follow-up care as follows:

- provide shelter and warmth;

- continue to assess the casualty's condition and react accordingly;

- collect the personal effects and protect them for hand-over to police or next-of-kin;

- make notes of the casualty's name and of the first aid given;

- if the casualty does not need medical aid, ensure that he is placed in the care of friends or relatives;

- assist in the hand-over to medical aid.

RESPONSIBILITIES OF A FIRST AIDER

When a First Aider goes to someone's aid, he undertakes to provide any assistance he can give safely and to remain on the scene until the casualty can be handed over to medical aid or some other authority. In this role of a Good Samaritan,[1] the First Aider is given certain protections under the law.[2] Therefore, he should not be overly concerned about legal liability.

A person has the right to accept *(consent)* or to refuse such help. A conscious adult or older child who agrees or makes no objection to your offer of help gives his consent. It is assumed that an unconscious person or a young child alone would consent to your help if he could. This is called *implied consent.* If a person refuses help, stay with him and keep a close eye on his condition until medical aid arrives. If he becomes unconscious and his life is endangered, do whatever is necessary to save his life.

SUSPECTED CHILD ABUSE

Be on the alert for signs of child abuse when giving first aid to children. Fractures in infants, unusually shaped bruises or burns and the child's apparent fear of the parent or babysitter should alert the First Aider. Insist upon medical attention for this child's injuries to permit a full medical assessment. If medical attention is refused and child abuse is strongly suspected, notify the local child welfare agency. Do not accuse a parent or babysitter of child abuse, but for the child's welfare, do not hesitate to report suspected cases.

---

1 Luke 10:30-36

2 Rozovsky, Lorne, *The Canadian Patient's Book of Rights* (Doubleday Canada Limited, Toronto, 1980) p.61. "These laws *(the law of the Good Samaritan)* have the effect of removing from the patient his fundamental right to sue the Good Samaritan for negligence. ... He *(the Good Samaritan)* can be held responsible only if he is "grossly negligent." *(Gross negligence is given a definition of "wanton and willful misconduct".)*

Notes

2

THE BODY
AND ITS FUNCTIONS

SYSTEMS OF THE BODY

The structure and functions of the body are easier to understand if they are considered as systems related to one another and dependent on one another. A basic knowledge of the skeletal, muscular, nervous, digestive, urinary, circulatory and respiratory systems is important in understanding injuries and illnesses and in giving correct first aid. These systems are so interrelated that injury to one system almost always results in injury to one or more of the others.

SKELETAL AND MUSCULAR SYSTEMS

The bones, which make up the framework of the body, form the skeletal system. The bones of the skeleton, together with the muscles attached to the bones, allow the body to move. The main functions of the skeleton are:

* to give the body shape and firmness;

* to act as levers to be operated by the attached muscles to enable the body to move; and

* to protect important organs in the head, chest and abdomen.

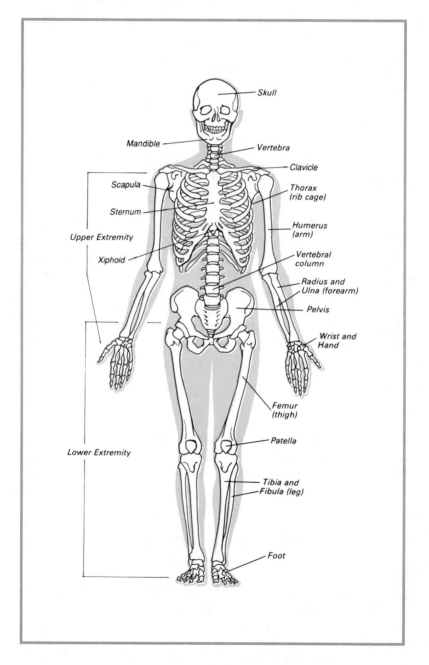

Fig. 2-1. The human skeleton.

JOINTS

Joints are formed where two or more bones come together. Some are fused joints and have little or no movement. Movable joints are held together with bands of strong tissue called **ligaments**, which allow limited movement in certain directions. Bone ends of movable joints are covered with smooth **cartilage** to reduce friction. A movable joint is enclosed in a tough tissue called the **capsule**.

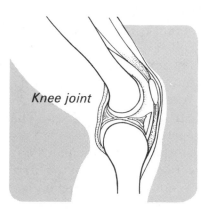

Fig. 2-2. A movable joint.

Joint injuries, such as sprains and dislocations, result when the bones are moved beyond their normal range. This causes stretching or tearing of ligaments and capsule *(see chap. 8 - Injuries to Bones and Joints)*.

SKULL

The skull *(cranium)* is the bony framework of the head. It is composed of numerous bones fused together to enclose the brain, eyes, inner ear, nose and the organs of the mouth. The lower jaw *(mandible)* is hinged on either side of the skull to permit movement for speaking and eating. The brain takes up most of the space in the skull.

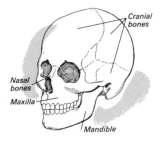

Fig. 2-3. The skull.

SPINE

The backbone *(vertebral column or spine)* is made up of thirty-three bones called vertebrae. A vertebra is a circular bone with an opening or passage immediately toward the back. The vertebrae are separated by pads of cartilage called discs. The circular opening in each vertebra is aligned to form a canal through which the spinal cord descends from the brain. Nerves extend out from the spinal cord through each side of the vertebrae to all parts of the body. The bones of the lower spine are fused, forming a large triangular bone called the sacrum.

Fracture or dislocation of the spine can cut or pinch the spinal cord, causing paralysis below the point of injury.

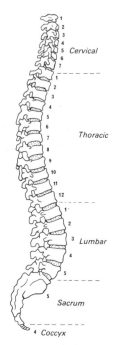

Fig. 2-4. The backbone (spine).

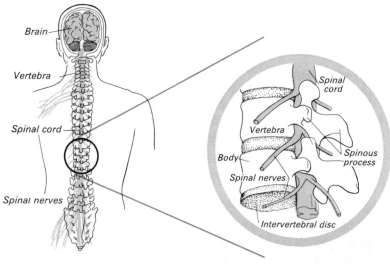

Fig. 2-5. The spinal cord.

Although nerve damage often occurs at the time of injury, it can also be caused or made worse by careless handling after the injury. This is the reason neck and back injuries must be treated in a special way and with the greatest care.

RIBS AND BREASTBONE

The rib cage consists of twelve pairs of curved bones connected to the spine at the back and curving around to form the chest. Ten pairs are connected to the breastbone *(sternum)* by cartilage. The remaining two pairs are not connected at the front. These are called floating ribs. The breastbone is a dagger-shaped bone that extends from the top of the rib cage to a point just above the pit of the stomach. The pointed, lower tip of the sternum *(xiphoid process)* can cause damage to internal organs if it is dislocated. The rib cage encloses the windpipe *(trachea)*, gullet *(oesophagus)*, lungs, the heart and major blood vessels. The ribs provide some protection to the organs of the upper abdomen — liver, spleen, stomach and kidneys.

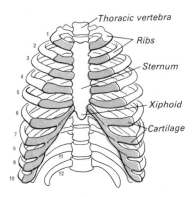

Fig. 2-6. Ribs and breastbone.

SHOULDERS AND UPPER LIMBS

The bones of the shoulder and upper limb are the collarbone *(clavicle)*, shoulder blade *(scapula)*, upper arm *(humerus)* the two bones of the forearm *(radius and ulna)* and the bones of the wrist and hand *(carpals, metacarpals and phalanges)*.

The collarbone con-
nects the breastbone to
the shoulder blade and
acts as a brace for the
shoulder. The shoul-
der blade is a flat, tri-
angular bone that lies
over the ribs at the
upper and outer part of
the back. It connects
with the collarbone and
forms a socket. The

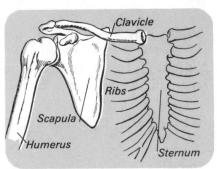
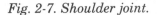

Fig. 2-7. Shoulder joint.

bone of the upper arm has a
ball-shaped end that fits into
the shoulder socket to form a
joint. Its lower end forms
part of the elbow joint. The
two bones of the forearm
connect with the upper arm
to complete the elbow joint.

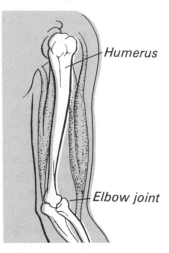

Fig. 2-8. Elbow joint.

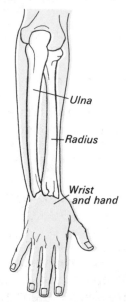

Fig. 2-9. Lower arm.

At their lower ends, the two
bones of the forearm con-
nect with the small bones of
the wrist to form the wrist
joint. The wrist connects
with the bones of the hand
to complete the upper limb.

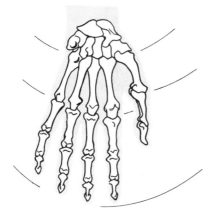

Fig. 2-10. Wrist and hand.

PELVIS AND LOWER LIMBS

The pelvis is a large basin-shaped bony structure formed by two hipbones joined together at the front and connected to the sacrum at the back. Each hipbone has a socket to receive the ball-shaped end of the thighbone *(femur)*. The pelvis supports the lower abdomen, and it protects the organs of the digestive, urinary and reproductive systems.

The bones of the lower limb are the thighbone, the kneecap *(patella)*, the two bones of the lower leg *(tibia and fibula)* and the bones of the ankle and foot *(tarsals, metatarsals and phalanges)*. These bones form movable joints at the hip, knee, ankle and toes.

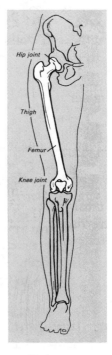

Fig. 2-11. Thighbone.

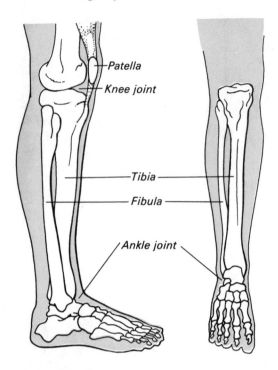

Fig. 2-12 . Lower leg and foot.

MUSCLES

Muscle is a special tissue that contracts by nerve stimulation. When several muscles work together, shortening and lengthening *(contracting and relaxing)*, parts of the body are made to move. There are two types of muscles:

- **voluntary muscles** are controlled directly by the brain. They contract and relax at the will of the individual. Most muscles of the skeleton are voluntary and are attached to bones by rope-like cords called **tendons**.

- **involuntary muscles** contract and relax rhythmically, regardless of the will of the individual. Two examples of this type are the muscle tissues of the heart and intestine.

THE NERVOUS SYSTEM

The nervous system consists of the brain, the spinal cord and the nerves. The brain takes up most of the space in the skull. The mass of nerve fibres that form the upper part of the spinal cord fills the opening at the base of the skull leading to the spine. Nerves spread out from the spine to reach all parts of the body.

Some nerves are called **motor nerves** because they stimulate movement; others are called **sensory nerves** because they transmit sensations of touch, taste and pain to the brain. Some nerve actions are caused by the will of the individual; others are involuntary and continuous. The involuntary nerves control such activities as heart action, breathing and digestion. Injury to nerves usually results in the loss of movement and sensation or the interference with an involuntary function of the life-support system.

The brain and the organs of hearing and sight are delicate and easily damaged. Head injuries that cause bleeding in the skull will result in pressure on the brain as the blood compresses brain tissue. Other head injuries can cause discharge or bleeding from the ears or changes in the reaction of the pupils of the eyes to light. Unconsciousness is a general effect of most brain injuries *(see chap. 6 - Unconsciousness).*

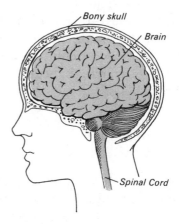

Fig. 2-13. The brain.

DIGESTIVE AND URINARY SYSTEMS

The digestive and urinary systems change food and drink into nourishment for the body and collect and dispose of solid and fluid waste matter. The organs of digestion, such as the gullet, stomach, bowel, liver, gallbladder and pancreas, are classified as either hollow or solid. If one of the hollow organs is ruptured or punctured, infection of the abdomen is caused by spillage of its contents. Because the solid organs have a rich blood supply, they bleed severely when damaged.

Similarly, the organs of the urinary system, consisting of the kidneys, ureters, urinary bladder and urethra, are classified as hollow or solid. Rupture of any of these organs is serious because of loss of blood or spillage of its contents.

CIRCULATORY SYSTEM

The main organs of the circulatory system are the heart, arteries and veins. The heart pumps blood into the arteries to carry it throughout the body, delivering oxygen (O_2) and nutrients. The blood collects carbon dioxide (CO_2) and other wastes and returns to the heart through the veins. The lungs, the major organs of respiration, play an important part in blood circulation by providing for the exchange of gases — exchanging carbon dioxide for oxygen through the thin walls of the air sacs *(alveoli)* in the lungs.

THE HEART

The heart is a hollow muscular organ located in the chest cavity behind the breastbone. This organ is divided into a right and left half, and each of these halves is further divided into a top and bottom section. The top section on each side is a collecting chamber *(right atrium and left atrium)*, the

bottom section on each side is a pumping chamber *(right ventricle and left ventricle).*
Valves separate the collecting and pumping chambers and separate each pumping chamber from its artery. These valves ensure that blood flows only in one direction. The healthy heart contracts and relaxes rhythmically, and the four chambers and their valves work together to keep blood moving to the lungs and throughout the body.

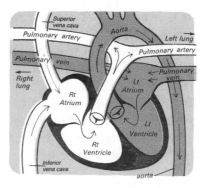

Fig. 2-14. The heart and large vessels.

CIRCULATION

Blood from the veins flows into the collecting chamber of the right side of the heart, which empties into the right pumping chamber. At the same time, blood is pouring into the collecting chamber on the left side from the two large veins of the lungs and empties into the left pumping chamber. When the lower chambers are filled, the valves from the collecting chambers close and the heart contracts, forcing blood out of both pumping chambers into the arteries. The blood from the right side is sent to the lungs, and that from the left side is pumped throughout the remainder of the body. The heart then relaxes and refills as the entire sequence is repeated.

PULSE

Each time the heart contracts or "beats", blood is pumped into the arteries, resulting in a pressure wave or pulse. This pulse can be felt with the fingertips where the arteries come near the skin. The normal pulse has a strong, steady rhythmic beat. The beats-per-minute *(rate)* varies with age and with exercise. The pulse rate of a healthy infant at rest varies from 80 to 140 beats per minute. The pulse rate of a healthy child at rest varies from 80 to 100 beats per minute. A healthy adult can have a resting pulse rate that varies from 50 to 100 beats per minute; the average is about 72. Resting pulse rates may be slower in athletes and older persons. Illnesses and injuries can cause the pulse strength to be bounding or very weak, the rate to be rapid or very slow and the rhythm to be erratic instead of regular.

You should know how to check a pulse to determine if it is normal, abnormal or absent. The most common places to take a pulse on an adult and child are at the neck *(carotid pulse)* and at the wrist *(radial pulse)*. In infants, check the pulse on the inside of the upper arm *(brachial pulse)*.

Carotid Pulse

The carotid pulse is preferred for pulse checks on an un-
conscious adult or child. To take a carotid pulse, locate the Adam's apple at the front of the neck with the tips of the index and middle finger. Slide the fingertips backward on the side nearest you to locate the large muscle at the side of the neck. Press gently with the fingertips between the muscle and the windpipe and a pulse will be felt. Count the number of beats in one minute, using a watch with a sweep second-hand. Note the rate, rhythm and strength of the beats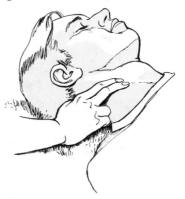

Fig. 2-15. Carotid pulse.

for abnormal signs. ***Do not feel for or compress both carotid arteries at the same time***. This could affect the blood supply to the brain and cause serious damage. Do not use your thumb when taking a pulse because it has a pulse of its own.

Radial Pulse

The radial pulse is checked on the palm side of the wrist above the thumb where the radial artery comes close to the surface. To take a radial pulse, place the fingertips on a point about 2.5 cm *(1 inch)* above the crease of the wrist and about 1.25 cm *(0.5 inch)* from the thumbside edge. Light pressure of the fingertips should be sufficient to feel the pulsations in the artery. Count the pulse beats, noting the strength and rhythm.

Fig. 2-16. Radial pulse.

Brachial Pulse

The brachial pulse is the most reliable and the most easily found in infants. It is located on the inside of the upper arm where the brachial artery crosses the bone of the upper arm. Place two fingertips on the inside of the upper arm and press lightly between the large muscle and the bone to feel the pulse.

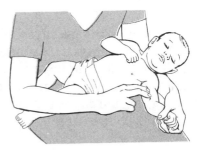

Fig. 2-17. Brachial pulse.

THE RESPIRATORY SYSTEM

The airway and lungs make up the respiratory system. It provides the mechanism for the exchange of gases in the circulatory system, removing carbon dioxide from the blood and replacing it with oxygen.

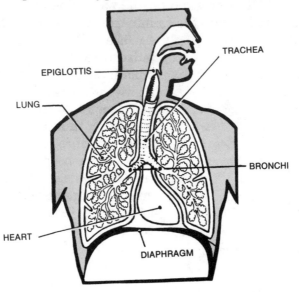

Fig. 2-18. The respiratory system.

AIRWAY

The airway is the passageway through which air passes to and from the lungs. It is made up of the mouth, nose and windpipe. The windpipe is in front of and parallel to the gullet, the passageway for food and drink. A flap-like valve *(epiglottis)* guards the entrance to the windpipe so that food or liquids do not enter.

LUNGS

The lungs are contained within the rib cage, one on each side of the chest. The lungs expand and contract with the movement of the ribs and diaphragm. The tissue of the tiny air sacs of the lungs is so thin that it allows gases to pass to and from the blood.

MECHANISM OF BREATHING

The body's need for oxygen causes the diaphragm and the muscles between the ribs *(intercostal muscles)* to expand the rib cage, enlarging the space in the chest. The diaphragm is a large dome-shaped muscular sheet located directly below the lungs between the chest and abdomen. When this muscle contracts, it becomes flat, creating more space within the rib cage and causing the lungs to expand. Air is drawn into the air sacs of the lungs where carbon dioxide, given off by the blood, is replaced by oxygen. This oxygen is carried by the blood to all parts of the body. The diaphragm and the muscles between the ribs then relax, causing the space within the rib cage to become smaller and air to be expelled from the lungs.

Normal Breathing Rates

Breathing is an automatic function. The rate of breathing is the number of breaths *(inhalations and exhalations)* in one minute. The normal breathing rate[1] varies for persons of different ages and sex, but the average rate for a healthy adult falls in the range of 10 to18 breaths per minute. The rates for children and infants are faster; 18 to 28 breaths per minute is considered normal for a five to seven year old and 41 to 55 breaths per minute is the normal range for an infant.[1]

---

1 *Respiration and Circulation.* Philip L. Altman and Dorothy S. Dittner, Editors for the series *Biological Handbooks.* The Federation of American Societies for Experimental Biology, Bethesda, Maryland, 1971 p. 42.

Notes

3

ARTIFICIAL RESPIRATION AND CARDIOPULMONARY RESUSCITATION

BREATHING EMERGENCIES

There are three conditions that must exist for breathing to supply adequate oxygen to the cells of the body. Think of them as the **ABC**s of breathing:

- **A**irway. It must be open to allow air to reach the lungs.

- **B**reathing. There must be adequate air exchange and oxygen in the air to supply the blood.

- **C**irculation. Blood flow must be sufficient to carry the oxygen to the tissues.

Causes of breathing emergencies can be grouped under three headings:

1. obstruction of the airway;

2. lack of oxygen in the environmental air; and

3. interruption of the heart-lung action.

When any of these occur, the body is deprived of oxygen, causing a condition called asphyxia *(unconsciousness caused by a lack of oxygen).* Artificial respiration must be started without delay. Seconds count! *If the brain is deprived of*

oxygen for more than four minutes, brain damage may result.

PREVENTION

Accidents that cause asphyxia can often be prevented by simple safety precautions. When rescuing a non-breathing casualty for example, take care that you do not become asphyxiated by the same accident situation.

Airway obstruction, caused by the tongue as it falls to the back of the throat, can be prevented in an unconscious person by placing him in the recovery position *(see chap. 6 - Unconsciousness)* . Airway obstruction by food and other objects can be prevented *(see chap. 4 - Choking)*. Supervise children constantly when they are playing in water to prevent drowning. Near drowning also causes an airway blockage by a muscular spasm that prevents water *(and air)* from entering the lungs.

Oxygen (O_2) in the air is displaced by other gases and fumes in enclosed areas. Carbon monoxide gas *(CO)* from combustion engine exhaust quickly displaces oxygen in the blood. Fumes in farm silos *(nitrogen dioxide — NO_2)* and manure gas *(hydrogen sulphide — H_2S)* in enclosed animal pens are particularly dangerous. All of these gases can kill. Ensure that work areas are well ventilated or wear a self-contained breathing apparatus and a lifeline if you must work in confined spaces in which there may be poisonous gases.

Heart and lung action can be interrupted by anything that interferes with normal brain and nerve functions. Such causes as drugs, poisons, electric current or brain injury, may interfere with the normal action of the lungs and heart. Damage to the heart muscle from a heart attack disrupts heart function. Injury to the chest wall from fractures or punctures will interfere with proper lung action. Be on the alert for any of these injuries that decrease proper exchange of gases and deprive the brain of oxygen. Be prepared to give appropriate first aid.

DIRECT METHODS OF ARTIFICIAL RESPIRATION

The direct methods — mouth-to-mouth, mouth-to-nose and mouth-to-mouth-and-nose — are the most effective first aid means of artificial respiration because:

- they provide the greatest volume of air to the lungs and come closest to natural breathing;

- they can be started immediately during rescue and continued while the casualty is moved to safety;

- they provide immediate warning if the airway is blocked;

- they are not tiring and can be carried out for long periods of time.

Artificial respiration, using one of the direct methods, consists of five simple manoeuvres:

1. Response assessment.

2. Breathing assessment.

3. Airway opening.

4. Lung ventilation.

5. Pulse assessment.

The application of each manoeuvre is described for an adult, as well as the variations in the technique and the precautions for its application to a child and an infant.

ADULT — CHILD — INFANT

Adult, child and infant are defined for the purpose of first aid so that the techniques of resuscitation can be varied correctly to minimize the risk of injury:

- adult — over the age of 8 years;

- child — from 1 year to 8 years of age;

- infant — 12 months of age or less.

RESPONSE ASSESSMENT

Assessing response is simply a way of determining if a person is unconscious or merely sleeping. Gently shake the person by the shoulders and call out to them to arouse them. If there is no response, assume that the person is unconscious and may not be breathing. If a head or neck injury is suspected, steady and support the head and neck before assessing responsiveness.

BREATHING ASSESSMENT

If a person is unconscious, there is a good chance that breathing may have stopped. Assess breathing immediately! Place your ear near the casualty's mouth and nose to listen for sounds of breathing. Your cheek should be close enough to feel air coming from the casualty's mouth and nose. Look toward the casualty's chest for any signs of movement. This assessment should take no more than 3 to 5 seconds. If you cannot detect any signs of breathing, assume that breathing has

Fig. 3-1. Check for breathing.

stopped. To minimize head and neck movement, assess breathing before opening the airway—not all unconscious casualties are in respiratory arrest.

AIRWAY OPENING

Fig. 3-2(a). Airway closed.

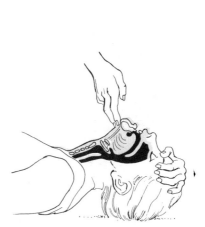

Fig. 3-2(b). Airway partially open.

Fig. 3-2(c). Airway open.

Airway opening techniques are best applied to a casualty who is lying on his back. Move the casualty onto his back, turning the head, neck and trunk as one unit to avoid twisting the neck and lower spine. There are two techniques recommended for opening the airway; head tilt—chin lift, and jaw thrust without head tilt.

Head Tilt—Chin Lift

The head tilt—chin lift method is the most effective way of opening the airway of a casualty who has no neck injuries. To apply this method, place one hand on the casualty's forehead and push backward. At the same time, place two fingers of the other hand under the bony part of the chin and lift upward. This will move the jaw forward and bring the tongue away from the back of the throat. This should open the airway, allowing air to enter the lungs.

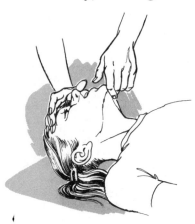

*Fig. 3-4. Head tilt—chin lift
- infant.*

Fig. 3-3. Head tilt—chin lift.

Take care when using the head tilt—chin lift on children and infants. If your fingers are not placed directly on the bony part of the chin, you may compress the soft tissue under the chin and block the airway. Tilt an infant's head gently; the neck is delicate and if it is stretched back too far, it could kink the airway and prevent air from entering the lungs. Overextending an infant's neck may also cause injury.

Jaw Thrust Without Head Tilt

The jaw thrust without head tilt method is used to open the airway of a casualty with a suspected neck injury. This method lifts the jaw forward, but does not tilt the head. This is to avoid damaging the spinal cord.

To apply the jaw thrust without head tilt, place the hands on each side of the casualty's face with the thumbs on the chin and the fingers under the bony angle of the jaw. Keep the head fixed between the palms of the hands to keep it from

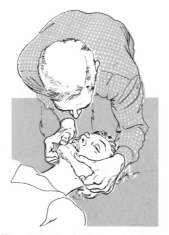

Fig. 3-5. Jaw thrust without head tilt - adult.

Fig. 3-6. Seal the nose with your cheek.

moving. Lift, using only the fingers, to move the jaw forward. This should bring the tongue away from the back of the throat and allow air to enter the lungs. Press with the thumbs on the chin to keep the mouth open.

To ventilate the lungs while using the jaw thrust without head tilt, cover the mouth

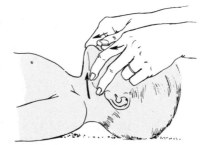

Fig. 3-7. Jaw thrust without head tilt - infant.

with your mouth and seal the nose with your cheek to prevent the escape of air.

LUNG VENTILATION

If opening the airway does not restore breathing, use your own breath to ventilate the lungs of a non-breathing person.

There is more than enough oxygen left in your exhaled air to keep another person alive if you breathe it into his lungs.

Rate and Depth of Breathing

Give breaths slowly to avoid forcing air into the stomach. If the stomach fills with air, artificial respiration becomes less effective and the casualty may vomit. Take from 1 to 1.5 seconds to give each breath and pause to allow the casualty to exhale.

The force used to give each breath depends on the size of the casualty. Breathe with just enough force to expand the chest. Adults usually need full breaths, but use light breaths for children and puffs of air for infants.

The rate of breathing should be as close as possible to normal breathing. The recommended rates of breathing are:

• adult — once every five seconds;

• child — once every four seconds;

• infant — once every three seconds.

Breathe into the casualty's lungs using one of the following direct methods of artificial respiration.

MOUTH-TO-MOUTH METHOD

To use the mouth-to-mouth method of artificial respiration, continue the chin lift with one hand and maintain the head tilt with the edge of the other hand. Use the thumb and forefinger of the hand on the forehead to pinch the nostrils closed to prevent air loss. Take a breath, cover the casualty's mouth with your mouth and breathe into his lungs. Release the seal at the nose, maintain the airway open and keep your face near the casualty's as you look, listen and feel for air being exhaled. This will confirm that the airway is not obstructed and that air is reaching the lungs.

Fig. 3-8. Mouth-to-mouth ventilation.

Fig. 3-9. Look for the fall of the chest.

MOUTH-TO-NOSE METHOD

If a casualty has injuries to his mouth or you cannot fully cover the mouth with yours, you can get air into his lungs by breathing through his nose.

Open the airway with the head tilt—chin lift, but close the mouth to make an airtight seal. Take a breath, cover the casualty's nose with your mouth and breathe through his nostrils into his lungs. Open the casualty's mouth to allow air to escape during exhalation. Keep your ear near the casualty's mouth as you look, listen and feel for air movement and the fall of the chest. If the lungs inflate, continue breathing for the casualty.

Fig. 3-10. Mouth-to-nose method.

MOUTH-TO-MOUTH-AND-NOSE METHOD

For infants and small children, the mouth-to-mouth-and-nose method is more effective because your mouth can cover both the mouth and nose at one time.

Fig. 3-11. Mouth-to-mouth - and nose.

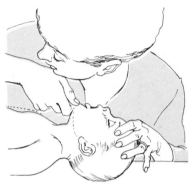

Fig. 3-12. Look for chest movement.

Open the airway, take a breath, cover the infant's mouth and nose with your mouth to make a tight seal. Breathe a puff of air into the lungs. Take your mouth away, but keep your face near as you look for movement of the chest and you listen and feel for air returning from the lungs. This will confirm that the airway is not obstructed and that ventilations can be continued.

Ventilation Attempt Fails

If the chest does not rise when you attempt to ventilate, reposition the head and increase the chin lift. Ensure tight seals at the mouth and nose and try again. If the chest still does not rise, you should suspect an airway obstruction and proceed with first aid for choking *(see chap. 4 - Choking).*

Gastric Distention and Vomiting

If the casualty's stomach becomes distended *(filled with air)* during artificial respiration, reposition the head and chin to improve the airway opening and breathe less forcefully. Continue ventilations, but do not attempt to expel the air from the stomach. This could cause vomiting.

If vomiting occurs during artificial respiration, turn the casualty over onto his side quickly to allow the vomitus to flow from his mouth and to prevent it from being breathed into the lungs. Wipe out the mouth quickly, return the casualty onto his back and resume artificial respiration.

PULSE ASSESSMENT

Assess the casualty's pulse during artificial respiration to make sure that oxygen is being carried by the blood throughout the body. Pulse assessments are made:

- after the two initial breaths;

- after one minute of artificial respiration; and

- every few minutes during artificial respiration.

A non-breathing person may have a pulse that is difficult to detect; it may be weak, slow, irregular or absent. Therefore, make a careful check of the carotid pulse on an adult or child and the brachial pulse on an infant *(see chap. 2 - The Body and its Functions)*. Take five to ten seconds to detect any sign of a pulse.

ARTIFICIAL RESPIRATION - SEQUENTIAL STEPS

To give effective artificial respiration, the five manoeuvres should be performed quickly and in the proper sequence. The steps of artificial respiration are:

1. **Establish unresponsiveness.** Gently tap the shoulder and shout, "Are you O.K.?" If there is no response ...

2. **Assess breathing.** Look, listen and feel for signs of breathing (3 to 5 seconds). If none of these signs is present ...

3. **Call out for help.** Shout or use any other method to attract the attention of anyone who may call medical aid and assist with first aid.

4. **Position the casualty.** Place the casualty on her back, supporting the head and neck, and turning the body as a unit.

5. **Open the airway.** Use either the head tilt—chin lift or the jaw thrust without head tilt to open the airway. While keeping the airway open ...

6. **Reassess breathing.** Look, listen and feel again for signs of breathing (3 to 5 seconds). Opening the airway may have restored spontaneous breathing. If no signs of breathing are detected ...

7. **Start artificial respiration.** Ventilate the lungs, giving two initial breaths. Maintain an open airway and ...

8. **Check the pulse.** Locate and assess the carotid pulse in adults and children or the brachial pulse in infants. Allow 5 to 10 seconds in the initial check to detect and

assess what may be a weak, slow pulse. If a pulse is detected ...

9. **Send for help**. Have someone call for medical aid. Ensure that they have all the needed information to pass on to the police or the emergency services dispatcher *(see chap. 1 - Principles and Practices)*. ***Do not leave a non-breathing casualty, whose heart is beating, to call medical aid.***

10. **Resume ventilations**. Ventilate the lungs every 5 seconds for an adult, every 4 seconds for a child and every 3 seconds for an infant. Look for movement of the chest and listen and feel with your cheek for air flow from the lungs after each breath.

11. **Reassess the pulse**. Reassess the carotid or brachial pulse after the first minute of artificial respiration *(5 seconds should be sufficient on recheck)* and every few minutes thereafter.

FOLLOW-UP CARE

When the casualty starts to breathe, place her in the recovery position *(see chap. 6- Unconsciousness)*. If neck injuries are suspected and the casualty must be left unattended, apply a cervical collar *(see chap. 8 - Injuries to Bones and Joints)* before carefully turning the casualty into the recovery position. The recovery position helps to maintain an open airway and it will help to prevent fluids and vomitus from being breathed into the airway.

Casualties who have experienced a breathing emergency must be monitored carefully in case further breathing difficulties arise. They should be taken to medical aid promptly.

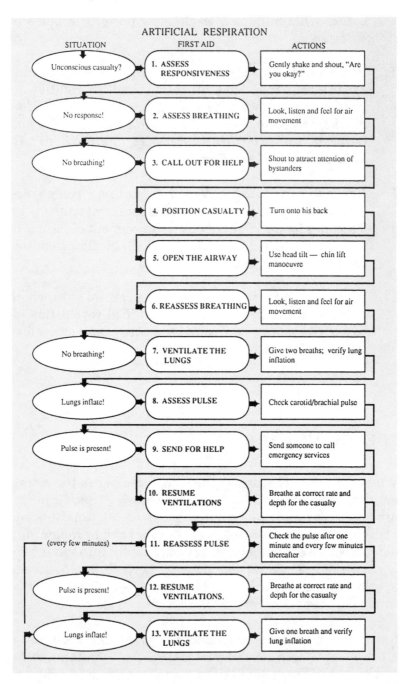

Fig. 3-13. Artificial respiration flowchart.

CARDIOPULMONARY RESUSCITATION (CPR)

CPR is a combination of two basic life-support techniques — artificial circulation *(cardio resuscitation)* and artificial respiration *(pulmonary resuscitation)* . The two techniques are combined to help a casualty who has stopped breathing and whose heart has stopped beating. If CPR is started without delay, a skilled rescuer can help to maintain life until medical aid is obtained.

The ABCs of CPR for a casualty who is not breathing and whose heart has stopped are to:

- open the **A**irway;

- restore **B**reathing;

- restore **C**irculation.

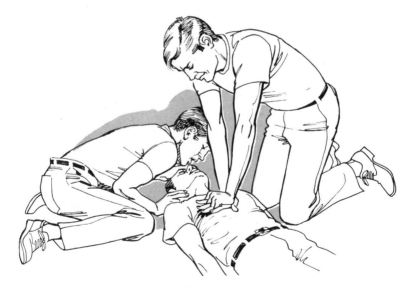

Fig. 3-14. Cardiopulmonary resuscitation.

ARTIFICIAL CIRCULATION

Artificial circulation is achieved by chest compressions. This is done by applying rhythmic, manual pressure to the lower half of the breastbone. The compressions increase the pressure within the chest, forcing blood out of the heart for circulation.

CPR should only be done by trained rescuers. It involves a combination of assessment skills and finely coordinated physical skills, which requires frequent manikin practice and retraining. Complete CPR procedures for adults, children and infants are contained in *First Aid Safety Oriented, Third Edition, 1990,* published by St. John Ambulance Canada.

4

CHOKING

Breathing emergencies that are caused by airway obstructions are called choking. Obstruction of the airway by swelling of the tissues of the throat caused by injury, disease or allergic reaction requires medical aid urgently. Choking from such causes as the tongue falling to the back of the throat and food lodged in the throat can be relieved by first aid measures. However, many of these mishaps can be prevented.

PREVENTION

Take special care when eating and drinking to ensure that solid foods are cut in small pieces and are well chewed before they are swallowed. Take care that drinks are not gulped when there is food in the mouth. Caution children not to run with food or other objects in their mouths. Keep small objects out of the reach of infants and supervise them closely.

RECOGNIZE CHOKING

Learn to recognize choking quickly so that you can relieve the obstruction before the condition becomes more serious. The choking person may clutch her throat, cough and wheeze when breathing, or her breathing may stop suddenly and she will fall unconscious. Watch for the person who suddenly coughs and leaves the table during a meal. She may be choking, but is leaving to avoid embarrassment. Go with her so that you can give first aid if it is needed.

Fig. 4-1. Sign of choking.

Partial and Complete Airway Obstruction

A partial airway obstruction allows some air to enter the lungs. You will recognize this by the casualty's attempts to cough. The degree of airway blockage is determined by the quality of air exchange:

- **good air exchange** is taking place when there is forceful coughing, even though there may be wheezing between coughs. Stand by ready to help. Encourage the person's efforts to clear the airway, but do not interfere.

- **poor air exchange** can be recognized by weak, ineffective coughing, a high-pitched crowing noise when inhaling and blueness around the mouth and nose. Give first aid to this person as if the obstruction is complete.

With a complete airway obstruction, the person cannot speak or breathe and is unable to cough. She will show signs of distress, such as clutching at the throat. Initial redness of the face *(congestion)* will change to blue *(cyanosis)* and she will soon become unconscious. First aid for choking must be started immediately.

FIRST AID MANOEUVRES FOR CHOKING

First aid for choking requires the use of one or more of the following five manoeuvres:

- abdominal thrusts;

- chest thrusts;

• back blows;

• finger sweeps or foreign body checks;

• lung ventilations.

The manoeuvres you use will depend on whether the casualty is conscious or unconscious, and whether it is an infant, a child, an adult, a woman in an advanced stage of pregnancy or a markedly obese person. Each manoeuvre is described in detail, including its application and on which casualty it should be used.

The appropriate manoeuvre, either alone or in combination with other manoeuvres, must be performed in rapid sequence to be effective. Back blows, chest thrusts and abdominal thrusts are potentially dangerous and must never be used with full force, except in an actual choking incident or on a manikin during training.

ABDOMINAL THRUSTS

The abdominal thrust (*also called Heimlich manoeuvre*) is more accurately described as a subdiaphragmatic thrust. This means that pressure is applied under the diaphragm to force air out of the lungs, creating an artificial cough. The abdominal thrust can be administered to a conscious adult or child who is standing or sitting, or to an unconscious adult or child who is lying on his back. The risk of causing internal injuries can be reduced if abdominal thrusts are properly applied. Abdominal thrusts must not be used on an infant, because they will cause serious injury. Their use is not recommended on a woman in an advanced stage of pregnancy nor on a markedly obese person, because of the difficulty of getting pressure under the diaphragm.

Abdominal Thrusts — Conscious Adult or Child

To give abdominal thrusts to a conscious adult or child who is standing or sitting:

* stand behind the casualty, reach under her arms and wrap your arms around her waist;

* locate the xiphoid process with the middle finger of one hand and the navel *(umbilicus)* with the middle finger of the other;

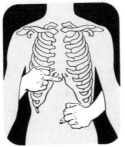

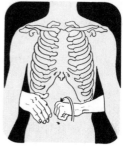

Fig. 4-2(a). Locate the xiphoid process and navel.

Fig. 4-2(b). Make a fist and rotate the hand.

* make a fist with the lower hand and roll it upward so that the thumb is against the abdomen, in the midline, just above the navel and well below the tip of the xiphoid;

* grasp the fist with the other hand and press upward quickly and forcefully, making each a distinct thrust with the intent of dislodging the obstruction.

Fig. 4-2(c). Grasp the fist with the other hand.

Fig. 4-2(d). Abdominal thrusts.

Give abdominal thrusts repeatedly to a conscious choking person until the obstruction is relieved or until the person becomes unconscious.

Abdominal Thrusts — Unconscious Adult or Child

To give abdominal thrusts to an unconscious adult or child:

* position the casualty on his back on a firm flat surface.

* kneel astride the casualty at the thighs or lower, so that the heels of your hands reach the upper abdominal area comfortably.

Fig. 4-3. Abdominal thrusts —lying down

- locate the xiphoid process with the middle finger of one hand and the navel with the middle finger of the other.

- let the hand at the xiphoid drop down so that the heel of the hand falls just above the navel.

- place the other hand on top of the first, ensuring that the fingers are parallel to the midline of the body. Keep the fingers interlocked to ensure that the pressure will be delivered only through the heels of the hands.

- thrust upward quickly and forcefully.

Give an unconscious casualty a series of six to ten distinct thrusts, each with the intent of dislodging the obstructing material.

Abdominal Thrusts — Self-Administered

A conscious person can administer abdominal thrusts to himself to assist his efforts to cough up a foreign body. To administer abdominal thrusts to yourself:

- make a fist and place it, thumb side in, in the midline just above your navel and well below the xiphoid process;

- grasp the fist with the other hand and press quickly and forcefully upward under the diaphragm;

Repeat these thrusts until the obstruction is dislodged.

The back of a padded chair or the edge of a counter or table can also be used for self-administered thrusts. Position the upper abdomen along the edge of the chair back, or along the edge of the counter or table. Press forcefully into the edge to apply pressure under the diaphragm. Repeat these abdominal thrusts until the obstruction is relieved.

CHEST THRUSTS

Chest thrusts are used when abdominal thrusts cannot be used effectively, such as on a woman in an advanced stage of pregnancy or a person who is markedly obese. Chest thrusts are also used on infants in order to avoid injury to internal organs. Chest thrusts can be administered to both the conscious and the unconscious casualty.

Chest Thrusts— Conscious Adult

To give chest thrusts to a pregnant or obese person who is standing or sitting:

- stand behind the casualty and reach under the armpits to position your hands mid-point on the chest;

- make a fist with one hand and position it, thumb side in,on the middle of the sternum, but well above the xiphoid process;

- grasp the fist with the other hand and pull backward forcefully to compress the chest.

Fig. 4-4. Chest thrusts — standing

Chest thrusts are given slowly and distinctly, each with the intent of relieving the obstruction. They are repeated until the airway is cleared or until the person becomes unconscious.

Chest Thrusts—Unconscious Adult

To deliver chest thrusts to a pregnant or obese person who is unconscious, place these casualties on their backs on a firm flat surface with their arms at their sides. Landmark the hands on the sternum to compress the chest.

Landmarking. To landmark for chest thrusts, kneel close to the casualty's chest near the shoulder. Use the hand nearest the casualty's feet for landmarking:

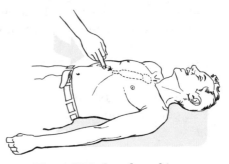

- locate the bottom edge of the casualty's rib cage nearest to you with the index and middle fingers of the landmarking hand;

Fig. 4-5(a). Landmarking — follow the ribs.

- run these fingers up the edge of the rib cage to the notch where the ribs meet the sternum;

- leave the middle finger in the notch and place the index finger above it on the lower end of the sternum;

Fig. 4-5(b). Landmarking — middle finger in the notch.

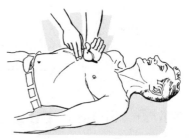

- place the other hand next to this index finger so that the heel of the hand runs along the length of the sternum with the fingers raised and pointing directly across the chest;

Fig. 4-5(c). Landmarking— position the hand.

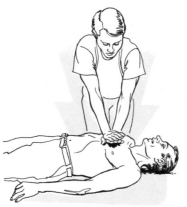

Fig. 4-5(d). Chest compressions.

• place the landmarking hand on top of the hand on the sternum with the fingers parallel and raised or interlocked to prevent any pressure being applied to the ribs.

Chest Compressions. With the hands correctly located on the sternum, you will achieve proper compressions by locking your elbows and bringing your shoulders directly over your hands so that your arms are vertical. Let your body weight apply pressure through the arms to the heels of the hands to depress the sternum to a depth of 3.8 cm to 5 cm *(1.5 to 2 inches)*.

If pressure is not applied straight down, the casualty's body will roll to one side and the effect of the chest compression will be lost.

Give an unconscious casualty six to ten chest thrusts in a series. Deliver each thrust slowly and distinctly with the intent that any one of them may dislodge the obstruction.

Chest Thrusts — Infant

Chest thrusts, in combination with back blows, are used to relieve airway obstruction in infants *(younger than 1 year)*, because abdominal thrusts may damage internal organs.

Landmarking. Chest thrusts are given to a choking infant with two fingers placed along the length of the sternum one finger's width below the nipple line. Position the fingers for chest compressions as follows:

- locate the centre of the sternum along an imaginary line between the nipples;

- place the tip of the index finger on the sternum just under this line and let the next two fingers fall in place next to the index finger;

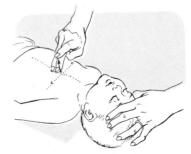

- raise the index finger, leaving the other two fingers in place ready to compress the infant's chest.

Fig. 4-6. Chest thrusts — infant.

Hold the infant on your thigh, while supporting the head and neck with the head lower than the trunk. Give four chest thrusts with sufficient pressure to depress the sternum 1.3 cm to 2.5 cm *(0.5 to 1 inch)*. Release the pressure between each thrust to allow the chest wall to return to its normal position, but keep the fingers in position to repeat the chest thrust.

BACK BLOWS

Back blows are only used in the care of a choking infant. To administer back blows:

- straddle the infant over your forearm, supporting the head by firmly holding the jaw. Keep the head lower than the trunk and rest your forearm on your thigh.

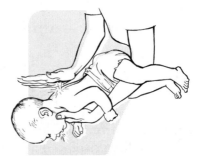

- position the open hand over the infant's back,

Fig. 4.7. Back blows — infant.

the heel of the hand between the shoulder blades and the fingers in line with the body.

- deliver four distinct blows with the heel of the hand to the area between the shoulder blades.

FINGER SWEEP/FOREIGN BODY CHECK

Finger sweep of the mouth of an adult or a foreign body check of the mouth of an infant and small child is a two-part manoeuvre that is used to dislodge and remove any loose matter that may be causing the obstruction.

Tongue-Jaw Lift. Place your thumb inside the mouth of the casualty to hold the tongue, while grasping the chin with the fingers. With the tongue and jaw held firmly between the thumb and fingers, lift the jaw. As the tongue is pulled forward, the foreign body may be dislodged, allowing air to get past to the lungs.

Finger Sweep/Foreign Body Check.   It may now be possible to remove the object with a "hooked" index finger as you sweep deeply into the mouth of an adult or older child. For infants and small children, use the tongue-jaw lift in an attempt to dislodge the object, but do not make blind finger sweeps of the mouth. Look into the mouth for any visible material and remove only foreign matter that you can see. Blind sweeps of an infant's or small child's mouth may accidentally push the obstructing material deeper into the throat.

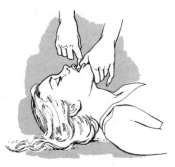

Fig. 4-8. Tongue-jaw lift and finger sweep.

LUNG VENTILATIONS

Open the airway and attempt to ventilate the lungs immediately following the finger sweep or foreign body check manoeuvre. If the chest rises, continue with artificial respiration until the casualty is breathing on his own *(see chap. 3 - Artificial Respiration and CPR)*. If the lungs do not inflate, continue with the manoeuvres to relieve the airway obstruction.

Fig. 4-9. Ventilate the lungs.

FIRST AID FOR CHOKING — SEQUENTIAL STEPS

When someone is choking, apply the manoeuvres appropriate to the casualty's state of consciousness, age and physical condition. These manoeuvres must be started quickly and applied in the proper sequence as detailed in the following steps.

CHOKING ADULT OR CHILD —CONSCIOUS

1. **Assess Obstruction.** As long as there is good air exchange, encourage coughing to relieve the obstruction. Stand by ready to help. Ask, "Are you choking?" When air exchange is poor or absent, consider the obstruction to be complete.

2. **Give Abdominal Thrusts.** Stand behind the casualty, reach under his arms and wrap your arms around the waist. Locate the xiphoid process with one hand and the

navel with the other. Position a fist just above the navel, but well below the xiphoid process. Grasp the fist with the other hand and give repeated quick upward thrusts until the obstruction is dislodged or until the casualty becomes unconscious.

CHOKING ADULT OR CHILD BECOMES UNCONSCIOUS

3. **Position the Casualty.** Ease the person to the floor or other firm, flat surface, on his back with his arms at his sides.

4. **Call Out/Send for Help.** Shout to attract bystanders and, if someone responds, send them to call emergency services. Provide all the information needed to ensure a prompt response to your call.

5. **Finger Sweep/Foreign Body Check.** Open the mouth with the tongue-jaw lift and attempt to dislodge or remove the obstructing material with a hooked finger. *Do not make blind finger sweeps of a child's mouth* Look and remove only foreign matter that can be seen.

6. **Open the Airway.** Use the head tilt — chin lift manoeuvre to open the airway.

7. **Ventilate the Lungs.** Attempt to ventilate the lungs. Watch the chest for any signs of expansion. This will indicate that air is getting past the obstruction and that artificial respiration should be continued. If the lungs do not inflate ...

8. **Give Abdominal Thrusts.** Kneel astride the casualty so that you can reach the upper abdomen comfortably with your hands. Locate the tip of the xiphoid with one hand, and the navel with the other. Place the heel of one hand just above the navel and the other hand on top.

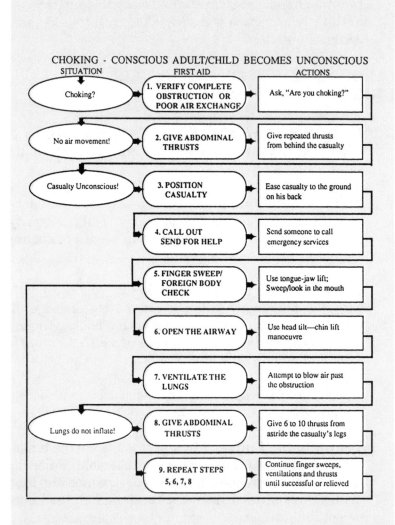

CHOKING - CONSCIOUS ADULT/CHILD BECOMES UNCONSCIOUS

SITUATION	FIRST AID	ACTIONS
Choking?	1. VERIFY COMPLETE OBSTRUCTION OR POOR AIR EXCHANGE	Ask, "Are you choking?"
No air movement!	2. GIVE ABDOMINAL THRUSTS	Give repeated thrusts from behind the casualty
Casualty Unconscious!	3. POSITION CASUALTY	Ease casualty to the ground on his back
	4. CALL OUT SEND FOR HELP	Send someone to call emergency services
	5. FINGER SWEEP/ FOREIGN BODY CHECK	Use tongue-jaw lift; Sweep/look in the mouth
	6. OPEN THE AIRWAY	Use head tilt—chin lift manoeuvre
	7. VENTILATE THE LUNGS	Attempt to blow air past the obstruction
Lungs do not inflate!	8. GIVE ABDOMINAL THRUSTS	Give 6 to 10 thrusts from astride the casualty's legs
	9. REPEAT STEPS 5, 6, 7, 8	Continue finger sweeps, ventilations and thrusts until successful or relieved

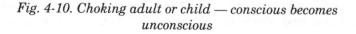

Fig. 4-10. Choking adult or child — conscious becomes unconscious

With the fingers raised or interlocked and in line with the centre line of the body, give 6 to 10 upward thrusts, each a separate and distinct movement.

9. **Repeat Finger Sweeps/Foreign Body Checks, Ventilations and Abdominal Thrusts.** Begin again at Step 5 and repeat finger sweeps/foreign body checks, ventilations and abdominal thrusts until the obstruction is relieved or until medical aid arrives on the scene.

FIRST AID FOR A CHOKING INFANT

Choking should be suspected in an infant who suddenly develops breathing difficulty associated with coughing, gagging or high-pitched noisy breathing sounds. If the breathing difficulty is due to an upper respiratory infection or to an allergic reaction, do not waste time trying to relieve the obstruction. Give artificial respiration and get this infant to a medical facility immediately.

Give first aid for choking to an infant when you see the choking incident occur or you strongly suspect a foreign body airway obstruction. Suspect an airway obstruction when attempts to ventilate the lungs of a non-breathing infant are unsuccessful and airway opening manoeuvres fail.

CHOKING INFANT — CONSCIOUS

1. **Assess Obstruction.** Encourage the infant's efforts if coughing is forceful and breathing is spontaneous. When breathing becomes ineffective with high-pitched crowing sounds or when breathing sounds are absent . . .

2. **Give Four Back Blows.** Straddle the infant over your forearm, supporting the head in your hand at a level lower than the trunk and supported on your thigh. Give four distinct blows with the heel of the hand between the infant's shoulder blades.

3. **Give Four Chest Thrusts.** Continue to support the head and neck as you turn the infant over onto his back, supported on your thigh with the head lower than the trunk. Place two fingers on the mid-sternum and give four distinct chest thrusts, compressing the chest 1.3 cm to 2.5 cm *(0.5 to 1 inch)* with each thrust.

4. **Repeat Back Blows and Chest Thrusts.** Continue giving series of four back blows and four chest thrusts until successful in dislodging the obstructing material or until the infant becomes unconscious.

CHOKING INFANT BECOMES UNCONSCIOUS

5. **Call Out/Send For Help.** Shout to attract bystanders and, if someone responds, send him to call emergency services. Provide all the information needed to ensure a prompt response to your call.

6. **Foreign Body Check.** Open the mouth with the tongue-jaw lift and attempt to remove any foreign matter that can be seen. *Do not make blind finger sweeps.*

7. **Open the Airway.** Use the head tilt — chin lift manoeuvre to open the airway.

8. **Ventilate the Lungs.** Attempt to ventilate the lungs. Cover the infant's mouth and nose with your mouth and give a light puff of air. Observe the chest for signs of expansion. If the chest expands, continue with artificial respiration. If the lungs do not inflate ...

9. **Give Four Back Blows.** Straddle the infant over your forearm, supporting the head in your hand at a level lower than the trunk. Rest your forearm on your thigh and give four distinct blows with the heel of the other hand between the infant's shoulder blades.

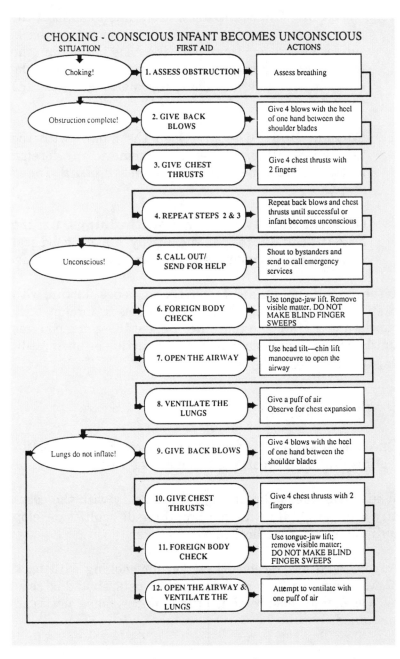

Fig. 4-11. Choking infant — conscious becomes unconscious.

10. **Give Four Chest Thrusts.** Continue to support the head and neck as you turn the infant over onto his back, supported on your thigh with the head lower than the trunk. Landmark two fingers on the midline of the sternum and give four chest thrusts to compress the chest 1.3 to 2.5 cm *(0.5 to 1 inch).*

11. **Foreign Body Check.** Open the mouth with the tongue-jaw lift and attempt to remove any foreign matter that can be seen. ***Do not make blind finger sweeps.***

12. **Open the Airway and Ventilate the Lungs.** Use the head tilt-chin lift to open the airway, make a good seal over the infant's mouth and nose and give a puff of air.

If the lungs do not inflate, repeat the sequence starting with Step 9, and give back blows, chest thrusts, foreign body checks and attempts to ventilate. Repeat these manoeuvres until successful in dislodging the obstruction or until medical aid arrives.

FOLLOW-UP CARE

Once the airway obstruction is relieved, continue with artificial respiration if breathing has not been restored.

When spontaneous breathing returns, stay with the casualty to ensure that no further breathing difficulties develop until he is under medical care.

Anyone who has received first aid for choking with back blows, chest thrusts and abdominal thrusts, should be seen by a doctor to ensure that other injuries have not been sustained.

5

WOUNDS AND BLEEDING

A wound is any damage to the tissues of the body, usually resulting in bleeding. Bleeding is the escape of blood from the vessels into surrounding tissue or externally from the body. Most wounds allow germs to enter the body, causing infection.

PREVENTION

Wounds often result from an unsafe act while using machinery, tools and equipment. Most of these accidents occur in the home during recreational and leisure activities. Such accidents can be prevented by a personal commitment to safety and by ensuring that family members work and play safely. Take special care to:

- ensure that safety guards are used when operating machine tools, such as hedge trimmers, chain saws, lawn mowers and sharp tools;

- ensure that machine tools are shut down and disconnected before servicing and that they are kept out of the hands of children and untrained adults;

- ensure that appropriate eye protection and hand protection is worn when operating machines;

- ensure that anyone involved in a hazardous sport wears the proper face and body protection equipment;

- operate motor vehicles, boats, tractors and recreational vehicles *(snowmobiles, motorcycles and all-terrain vehicles etc.)* in a safe manner.

DRESSINGS AND BANDAGES

First aid for wounds requires the use of dressings and bandages, either commercially prepared or improvised from readily available materials.

DRESSINGS

A dressing is a protective wound-covering used to control bleeding and to decrease the risk of infection. The ideal dressing should be:

- **germ free** *(sterile)* or at least clean.

- **absorbent**, so that it will soak up blood and other liquid discharges.

- **thick, soft and compressible**, so that bandage pressure will be evenly distributed over the wound area.

- a **material that will not stick** to the wound. Gauze, cotton, towels or sanitary pads are suitable, but woollen materials or loose absorbent cotton should be avoided.

Dressings may be improvised, but commercially prepared dressings should be part of every first aid kit. Three examples of these are:

- **adhesive dressings**. These sterile dressings are prepared with their own adhesive strips and are sealed in a paper covering. Adhesive dressings vary in size and are used primarily in first aid for small wounds with slight bleeding.

- **pressure dressings**. These large sealed, sterile dressings consist of a pad of absorbent cotton covered with layers of gauze with an attached roller bandage. The roller bandage is used to secure it firmly. Pressure dressings are used primarily to control severe bleeding.

- **gauze dressings**. Gauze material, usually folded into squares of various sizes, are sealed in paper coverings and sterilized. Any number can be applied to a wound and secured in place with a triangular or roller bandage.

BANDAGES

A bandage is any material that is used:

- to hold a dressing in place;

- to maintain pressure over a wound;

- to provide support for a limb or joint; and

- to immobilize parts of the body.

Commercially prepared triangular bandages or roller bandages should be in all first aid kits, but bandages may be improvised from neckties, scarves, belts or torn cloth strips.

THE TRIANGULAR BANDAGE

Triangular bandages are made by cutting a one-metre square of cloth from corner to corner to produce two triangular pieces. To simplify the instructions for the application of the triangular bandage, its parts are named as follows:

- the **BASE**, the longest side of the triangle;

- the **ENDS**, the ends of the base;

- the **POINT**, opposite the base; and

- the **SIDES**, the edges between the **ENDS** and the **POINT**.

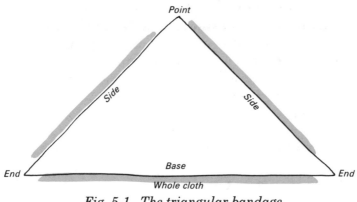

Fig. 5-1. The triangular bandage.

A triangular bandage may be applied as:

• a **whole cloth**. Opened to its fullest extent, it may be used for slings or to hold large dressings in place.

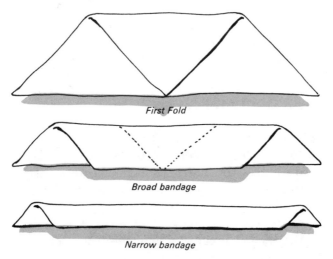

Fig. 5-2. The broad and narrow bandages.

• a **broad bandage**. Bring the **POINT** to the centre of the **BASE** and fold in half again from the top to the **BASE** to form a broad bandage. Use it to hold splints in place or to apply pressure evenly over a large area.

The broad bandage can be used for most applications unless its width puts pressure on a fracture site or the procedure specifically calls for a narrow bandage.

- a **narrow bandage**. Fold a broad bandage in half from the top to the **BASE** to form a narrow bandage. Use it to secure dressings in place. The narrow bandage may be more suitable for holding splints on small children.

RING PAD

Use a narrow bandage to form a loop around one hand by wrapping one **END** of the bandage twice around the four fingers. Pass the other **END** through the loop, wrapping it around and around until the entire bandage is used and a firm ring is made. It may be necessary, when making a larger ring, to tie a second narrow bandage to the first and to continue wrapping it through the loop to make a large, firm ring.

Fig. 5-3. Preparing a ring pad.

Use the ring pad to apply pressure around a wound to control bleeding when direct pressure cannot be applied, as in the case of a wound with an embedded object or a protruding bone. Ring pads of varying sizes should be made up in advance and kept in first aid kits ready for use.

THE REEF KNOT

The reef knot is recommended for tying bandages and slings because it is flat and more comfortable than other knots. It will not slip, but can be loosened easily.

To tie a reef knot, hold the ends of the bandage, one in each hand. Lay the end from the right hand over the one from the left hand and pass it under to form a half-knot. This will transfer the ends from one hand to the other. The end now in the left hand should be laid over the one from the right and passed under to form another half-knot. This will look like two intertwined loops that can be tightened by pulling one loop against the other or by pulling on the ends only.

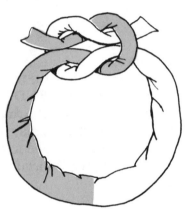

Fig. 5-4. The reef knot.

Remember the sequence for tying a reef knot by memorizing the following phrase: ***Right over left and under, left over right and under.***

If the end and the shank on one side of the knot are pulled away from each other, the knot will loosen easily and the other end can be slipped off.

Tie bandage knots so that they do not cause discomfort by pressing on skin or bone, particularly at the site of a fracture or at the neck when used to secure a sling. If the knot must be tied at a spot that may cause discomfort, place soft material underneath it as padding. Tuck knot ends away so they do not get caught or pulled when the casualty is moved.

APPLYING THE TRIANGULAR BANDAGE

Triangular bandages can be used to hold dressings in place and to apply pressure to various parts of the body.

Head Bandage

To hold dressings to the head:

* stand behind the casualty.

* use a triangular bandage as a whole cloth with a narrow hem folded along its **BASE**.

* place the centre **BASE** on the midpoint of the forehead, close to the eyebrows;

* bring the **POINT** over the top of the head to cover the dressing, and let it fall to the back of the head;

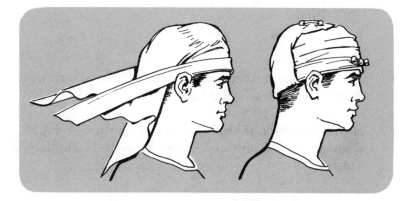

Fig. 5-5. Bandage for holding dressings on the scalp.

* bring the **ENDS** around the back of the head, crossing over the **POINT**, and continuing around the head to tie off low on the forehead;

- steady the head with one hand, and draw the **POINT** down to put the desired pressure on the dressings;

- fold the **POINT** up toward the top of the head and secure carefully with a safety pin.

Elbow and Knee Bandage

The procedures for holding dresssings on the elbow and knee are much the same:

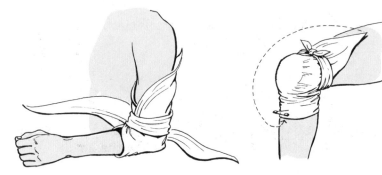

Fig. 5-6. Bandaging the elbow.   *Fig. 5-7. Bandaging the knee.*

- use a triangular bandage as a whole cloth with a narrow hem folded along its **BASE**;

- place the centre **BASE** on the forearm to bandage an elbow or on the shin below the kneecap to bandage a knee;

- position the **POINT** upward and over the dressing;

- bring the **ENDS** around the limb, crossing over in front of the elbow or at the back of the knee;

- bring the **ENDS** up and tie off over the **POINT** on the upper part of the limb;

- draw the **POINT** up through the tie to put the desired pressure on the dressings;

- fold the **POINT** downward and secure it on the lower part of the bandage with a safety pin.

Open Hand and Foot Bandage

To hold dressings on the open hand or foot:

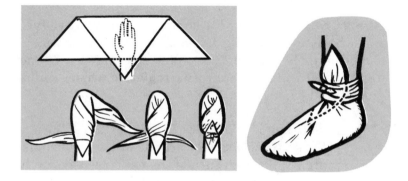

Fig. 5-8. Bandaging the open hand.   *Fig. 5-9. Bandaging the foot.*

- use a triangular bandage as a whole cloth placed on a flat surface with the **POINT** away from the casualty;

- place the open hand or foot on the triangular bandage with the fingers or toes toward the **POINT**, leaving sufficient bandage at the wrist or ankle to enclose the part;

- bring the **POINT** up and over the hand or foot to rest on the wrist or lower leg;

- bring the **ENDS** up and around the wrist or ankle, crossing over the **POINT** and repeating turns around the limb to use up any extra bandage before tying it off;

- draw the **POINT** through the tie to apply pressure to the dressings;

- fold the **POINT** downward and secure it with a safety pin.

ROLLER BANDAGE

The roller bandage, either the clinging or open-weave type, can also be used for holding dressings in place over a wound. It should be applied so that it is comfortable and firm, but not so tight that it will interfere with circulation when swelling of the injured part occurs.

To apply a roller bandage in a simple spiral, start at the narrow part of the limb and wrap toward the wider part to make it more secure. Make each turn of the bandage overlap the previous turn. Anchor the bandage at the first turn, as follows:

- place the end of the bandage on a bias at the starting point;

- encircle the injured part, allowing the corner of the bandage end to protrude;

- fold the the protruding tip of the bandage over the first turn and secure it in place with the next turn;

Fig. 5-10. Simple spiral bandage.

- continue to encircle the limb, overlapping each turn.

Secure the end of the roller bandage with tape or a safety pin.

FIGURE-8

A figure-8 is a method of applying a bandage to immobilize the ankles and feet, to apply a splint to the sole of the foot, or to support an injured ankle.

To apply a figure-8 to immobilize the ankles and feet:

- position a broad or narrow bandage under the ankles;

- bring the **ENDS** up and cross them over the ankles;

- draw the **ENDS** firmly around the bottom of the feet at the arch;

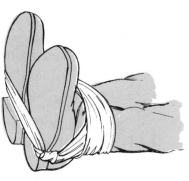

Fig. 5-11. The figure-8

- tie off on the edge of the shoe on the uninjured side.

SLINGS

Slings provide support and protection for the upper limbs. They may be used to elevate or immobilize a limb or to transfer its weight from one side of the body to the other.

ARM SLING

The arm sling supports the forearm and hand when there are injuries to the upper limb or ribs. To apply the arm sling:

- support the forearm across the chest, with the wrist and hand slightly higher than the elbow and the limb held slightly away from the chest;

• place a triangular bandage as a whole cloth between the forearm and the chest with its **POINT** extending beyond the elbow;

• bring the upper **END** over the casualty's shoulder on the uninjured side and around the neck to rest on the collarbone of the injured side;

Fig. 5-12. The arm sling.

• support the forearm, while you bring the lower **END** over the hand and forearm, and tie it off with the other **END** so that the knot rests in the hollow above the collarbone;

• bring the **POINT** around to the front of the elbow, and secure it to the sling with a safety pin or twist it into a "pigtail" and tuck it inside the sling.

Expose the fingers so that the fingernails can be checked for any signs of loss of circulation *(see chap. 8 - Injuries to Bones and Joints)*. White or blue fingernails and cold fingers are indications that circulation to the hand is affected and bandages around the limb should be loosened.

ST. JOHN TUBULAR SLING

The St. John tubular sling is used to support the hand and forearm in a well-elevated position and to transfer the weight of the upper limb from one side to the other. It is used in cases of wounds of the hand and for injuries to the shoulder and collarbone.

To apply a St. John tubular sling:

• support the forearm on the injured side across the chest so that the fingers rest on the collarbone of the opposite shoulder.

• place a triangular bandage as a whole cloth over the forearm and hand with its **POINT** extending beyond the elbow, its **BASE** in line with the side of the body and its upper **END** over the uninjured shoulder This **END** may be tucked under the hand to hold it in place.

Fig. 5-13. St. John tubular sling.

• support the forearm and ease the **BASE** of the bandage under the elbow, forearm and hand with a smooth sweeping motion.

• bring the lower **END** diagonally across the casualty's back and over the shoulder on the uninjured side.

• gently adjust the height of the arm as you tie off the **ENDS** so that the knot rests in the hollow above the collarbone on the uninjured side.

- tuck in the **POINT** between the forearm and the sling to form a pocket for the elbow and secure with a safety pin. If a safety pin is not available, the **POINT** may be twisted into a "pigtail" and tucked inside the sling.

COLLAR AND CUFF SLING

The collar and cuff sling is formed of two parts; a cuff around the wrist and a collar around the casualty's neck. It may be made from one or two triangular bandages, depending on the desired position of the arm or on how much the elbow can be bent. It is used to support the arm in an extended position when there are injuries to the elbow or shoulder that limit the movement of these joints.

To apply a collar and cuff sling:

- place the centre of a narrow triangular bandage on the forearm, letting the **ENDS** fall on either side, one near the wrist and one near the elbow to form a long diagonal;

- bring one **END** around the forearm and pass it under the centre to form a loop around the arm;

- bring the other **END** around the forearm in the opposite direction and pass it under the centre to form another loop;

Fig. 5-14(a). Making the cuff.

- bring both **ENDS** up to form a cuff around the wrist, keeping it wrinkle-free and fairly loose so that it supports the wrist comfortably;

- bring the **ENDS** around the casualty's neck and tie off so that the knot rests in the hollow above the collarbone on the injured side.

Fig. 5-14(b). Collar and cuff sling.

If additional length is needed to allow the arm to remain extended, tie the **END** of another narrow triangular bandage to one **END** of the first. Bring it around the casualty's neck and tie off the other two **ENDS** so that the arm is positioned at the desired level.

IMPROVISED SLINGS

Improvise slings by:

- placing the hand inside a buttoned jacket;

- using a scarf, belt, necktie or other item of clothing looped around the neck and the injured limb;

- pinning the sleeve of the shirt or jacket of the injured limb to the clothing in the desired position;

- turning up the lower edge of the casualty's jacket over the injured limb and pinning it to the upper part of the garment.

BLEEDING

SIGNS AND SYMPTOMS

Signs and symptoms of bleeding can be slight or severe, depending on the rate of bleeding and the amount of blood loss. Severe loss of blood will result in the following signs and symptoms that also indicate the progress of shock:

- restlessness and apprehension;

- pale, cold and clammy skin;

- rapid pulse, gradually becoming weaker;

- faintness and dizziness;

- thirst and nausea;

- shallow breathing, yawning, gasping for air.

First aid for shock is detailed in chapter 7.

CONTROL OF BLEEDING

The body has natural defences against bleeding. Damaged blood vessels constrict to reduce blood flow. Blood pressure drops as bleeding continues, reducing the force of blood flow. Blood will clot as it is exposed to air to form a seal at the wound. You can help the body to stop external bleeding by:

- **direct pressure**. Pressure on the wound, applied directly with the hand over a dressing, is the most effective way to control bleeding. Clots cannot form until bleeding is controlled.

- **elevation.** When a bleeding part is raised above the level of the heart, the blood is forced to flow upward, and the pressure is reduced.

- **rest**. When the casualty is placed at rest in a sitting or lying position, blood pressure is reduced and bleeding slows down.

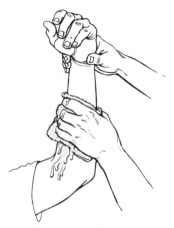

Fig. 5-15. Applying direct pressure and elevation.

Severe Bleeding

Bring severe bleeding under control quickly to prevent the loss of blood and to slow the progress of shock:

- apply a dressing over the wound if one is available, but do not waste time. If none is available, use the bare hand to maintain pressure. If dressings become blood-soaked, do not remove them, because this may disturb blood clots that have already formed. Add more dressings and increase the pressure.

- elevate the limb. Increase elevation until bleeding is brought under control.

When bleeding is brought under control, add more dressings if needed and bandage them securely to maintain pressure. Immobilize a limb in an elevated position if the injuries permit.

Slight Bleeding

Minor cuts and scrapes will cause slight bleeding, which will either stop of its own accord or can be controlled easily. To give first aid for wounds with slight bleeding:

- clean dirt away from the wound, washing it with clean water if possible and drying the area by wiping away from the wound.

- cover the wound with a sterile dressing, and hold it in place with a bandage. An adhesive dressing may be all that is needed to cover small wounds.

- place the casualty at rest, and elevate the bleeding part if possible.

CONTROL OF INFECTION

All wounds are contaminated to some degree. Prevent further contamination by taking the following precautions when time and conditions permit:

- wash your hands with soap and water before dressing the wound.

- do not cough or breathe directly over a wound.

- wash away any visible dirt from the wound and clean the surrounding skin with soap and water. Take care to swab away from the edges of the wound with clean gauze swabs.

- do not touch the wound with the fingers or touch the side of the dressing that will be placed on the wound.

- cover the wound promptly with a dressing that is sterile or at least clean.

Contaminated wounds may become infected. Infection in a wound can be recognized by reddening around the wound or red streaking away from the wound. The skin may be hard, swollen and warmer than normal to the touch. An older infection may show a yellow-green discolouration or a discharge as a result of the accumulation of pus. There is little you can do and medical care should be sought.

WOUND CARE

The aims of wound care are to stop the bleeding and prevent infection. Dressings, secured firmly over a wound, help achieve these aims.

WOUNDS OF THE HAND

Wounds of the palm of the hand usually cause severe bleeding because many blood vessels may be damaged. Crush injuries of the hand involve damage to bones and joints as well as soft tissues. These wounds require immobilization as well as dressings *(see chap. 8 - Injuries to Bones and Joints).*

If the wound is across the palm *(transverse)* and the fingers can be bent, give first aid as follows:

* cover the wound with a thick pad of dressings;

* bend the fingers over the pad to make a fist and to put pressure on the wound;

* bandage the clenched hand by placing the centre of a narrow triangular bandage on the inside of the wrist and bring the

Fig. 5-16(a). Care of a wound in the palm of the hand.

*Fig. 5-16(b). Secure with a
narrow bandage.*

ENDS around the back of the hand diagonally to cross over the fingers;

* bring the **ENDS** around the wrist to use up excess bandage and tie them securely;

* elevate and support the limb in a St. John tubular sling.

WOUNDS WITH EMBEDDED OBJECTS

Objects embedded in a wound, such as glass or a knife, should not be pulled out. This may cause further injury and increase bleeding. Dress and bandage the wound so that the object is stabilized without putting direct pressure on it.

If the embedded object is small or does not protrude too far, the wound should be dressed as follows:

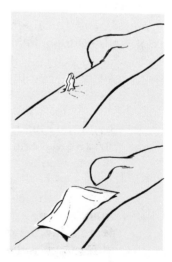

* "tent" dressings over the wound so that no pressure is applied to the object.

* make a ring pad large enough to surround the embedded object and the wound;

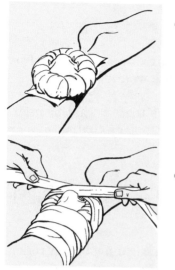

- place the ring pad over the dressings, ensuring that it clears the embedded object and that the dressings do not press on the object;

- secure the ring pad in place with a narrow bandage;

Fig. 5-17. Care of a wound with an embedded object .

- immobilize or support the limb to reduce movement.

If the embedded object protrudes too far to allow dressings over the wound:

- place dressings around the base of the object to cover the wound;

- build up around the object with bulky dressings to keep it from moving;

- bandage the dressings in place with a narrow bandage, taking care that pressure is not exerted on the object.

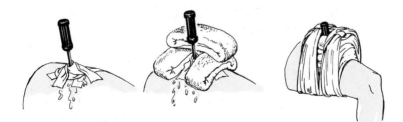

Fig. 5-18. Stabilizing a long embedded object.

BLEEDING GUMS

Bleeding from the gums occurs after tooth extraction or from jaw injuries. Give first aid for these wounds as follows:

*   place a gauze pad firmly on the tooth socket or injury site, using a pad thick enough to keep the teeth apart when biting;

*   instruct the person to bite on the pad and to support the chin with the hands until the bleeding stops, usually in 10 to 20 minutes;

*   seek medical advice if the bleeding cannot be controlled.

Do not rinse the mouth after bleeding has stopped as it may dislodge clots and restart bleeding. Care for knocked-out teeth as amputated tissue *(see page 89)*.

BLEEDING TONGUE OR CHEEK

Bleeding from the tongue or cheek should be stopped by compressing the wound between the finger and thumb, using a sterile dressing or clean cloth.

BLEEDING SCALP

Bleeding from the scalp is often severe and may be complicated by a fracture of the skull or an embedded object. When giving first aid for these wounds, avoid probing and contaminating the wound. Take particular care to:

*   clean away loose dirt;

*   apply a sterile dressing large enough to extend well beyond the edges of the wound and bandage it firmly in place;

- if there is an embedded object, apply a large ring pad over the dressing to maintain pressure around but away from the wound;

- if there is a suspected underlying skull fracture, use a thick, compressible, soft dressing instead of a ring pad and hold it in place with a head bandage;

- transport the casualty to medical aid.

NOSEBLEEDS

Nosebleeds may occur without apparent cause. They are more often caused by blowing the nose, by direct injury as in a broken nose, or by indirect injury such as a fractured skull *(see chap. 8- Injuries to Bones and Joints)*. Give first aid for nosebleeds as follows:

- place the casualty in a sitting position with the head held slightly forward;

- instruct the casualty to pinch the nostrils closed with the thumb and index finger for about 10 minutes;

- loosen clothing around the person's neck and chest if it is uncomfortably tight.

Instruct the casualty to breathe through his mouth and not to blow the nose for several hours after bleeding has stopped so that blood clots will not be disturbed. If bleeding does not stop with first aid, or if bleeding recurs, get medical aid.

WOUNDS OF THE ABDOMINAL WALL

Wounds of the abdomen may be open or closed. Closed wounds are those in which internal abdominal tissues are damaged but the skin remains intact. Open abdominal wounds are those in which the skin is broken. Open abdominal wounds may gape and must be prevented from opening wider by positioning the casualty with head and shoulders slightly raised and supported, and knees raised and supported. The method of dressing this type of wound depends on whether or not internal organs are protruding:

- if **no organs protrude**, apply a dressing to the wound and bandage firmly.

- if **internal organs protrude**, do not attempt to reinsert them. Cover the wound with a large moist gauze dressing or a soft clean moist towel and bandage loosely.

Do not give anything by mouth. Support the abdomen with broad bandages in case the casualty coughs or vomits. Transport to medical aid as quickly as possible.

CARE OF AMPUTATED TISSUE

Completely or partially amputated parts must be preserved, regardless of their condition, and taken to the medical facility with the casualty.

A **partially amputated part** should be:

- kept as near as possible to its normal position;

- covered with sterile gauze dressings, bandaged and supported;

- kept cool, but dry, with an ice bag applied outside the bandage.

A **completely amputated part** should be:

- wrapped in a clean, moist dressing, sealed in a clean watertight plastic bag labelled with the time and date this was done;

Fig. 5-19. Care of the amputated part.

- placed in another plastic bag or container partially filled with ice;

- transported with the casualty to a medical facility.

Keep amputated parts cool and moist. Do not use any antiseptic solutions and do not attempt to clean them in any way.

To care for a **knocked-out tooth**:

- do not handle the tooth by the root;

- gently replace the tooth in the socket if possible, otherwise, place it in moistened gauze or a cup of water;

- seek medical or dental aid quickly for best chance of reimplantation.

INTERNAL BLEEDING

Internal bleeding from injuries to organs inside the body, such as in the skull, chest and abdominal area, is very serious and may result in death. Internal bleeding is often concealed, but it can sometimes be recognized by blood coming from the nose, mouth and ears, or by the signs and symptoms of shock. There is little in first aid that can be done to control internal bleeding. The casualty needs medical aid as quickly as possible. While awaiting the arrival of an ambulance or on the way to a hospital make the casualty as comfortable as possible:

- place the conscious casualty at rest in the position best suited to his injuries and to slow the progress of shock as described in chapter 7 - *The Shock Position*;

- if the casualty is unconscious, place him in the recovery position because vomiting may occur *(see chap. 6 - Unconsciousness);*

- loosen tight clothing;

- keep the casualty warm;

- talk to the casualty. Tell him what you are doing and reassure him that help is on the way, or that he will soon be under medical care;

- do not give the casualty anything by mouth; wet his lips if he complains of thirst, but do not give anything to eat or drink.

Penetrating Wounds of the Chest

Penetrating wounds of the chest are very serious because of the severe blood loss and a possible lung collapse. Collapse of the lung can be caused by air as it enters the chest and fills the space between the chest wall and the lung. The lung collapses under the pressure of the air and is ineffective for breathing. The sound of air being sucked in during inspiration and bloodstained bubbles at the wound on expiration will confirm that it is a penetrating wound. The casualty may also cough up frothy blood. Impaired breathing and loss of blood will result in severe shock.

Stop the flow of air into the chest cavity quickly by applying an airtight covering of plastic or foil. Tape this dressing on three sides to create a flutter-type valve. When the casualty inhales, the dressing will seal the wound preventing air from entering the chest cavity. When the casualty exhales, the flutter valve will open allowing the air in the chest cavity to exit through the wound. This will prevent a build up of air in the chest cavity which could cause lung collapse. If there is an embedded object, do not remove it. Place dressings around the object and try to create a flutter-type valve. Support the arm on the injured side in a St. John tubular sling.

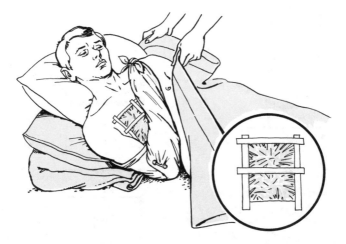

Fig. 5-20. Care of a penetrating wound of the chest.

Monitor breathing. Transport the casualty on a stretcher in a semisitting position inclined toward the injured side.

Puncture Wounds

Puncture wounds may not produce much external bleeding, but you should suspect internal bleeding, particularly if the wound is in the chest or abdomen. Some puncture wounds, such as those from a gunshot, may have both an entry and an exit wound. Such wounds cause internal tissue damage and severe bleeding. All puncture wounds must be considered serious because of the possibility of damage and contamination deep in the wound. Control bleeding, care for the wounds, and transport the casualty to medical aid.

Crush Injuries

Crush injuries from the weight of masonry, machinery or other heavy objects cause extensive damage to the tissues of

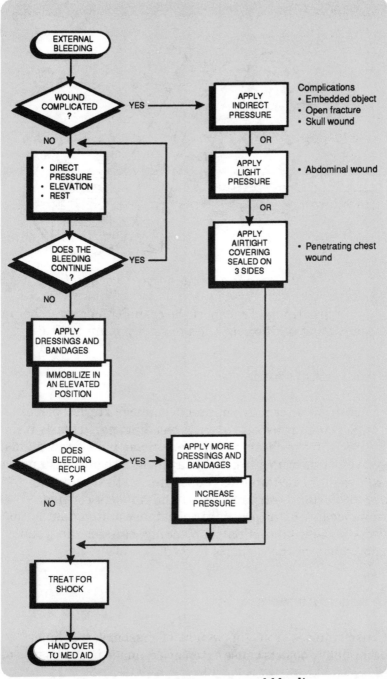

Fig. 5-21. Care of severe external bleeding.

the limbs or of the whole body. Such injuries may be complicated by fractures (*see chap. 8 - Injuries to Bones and Joints*)
and by ruptures of internal organs.

Shock, resulting from blood loss, is a serious complication of
crush injuries. Even though the signs and symptoms of
shock may not be apparent when the casualty is extricated
from the site of the accident, start first aid immediately to
lessen the severity of shock (*see chap. 7 - Shock*). First aid for
wounds and fractures will stop bleeding and relieve pain,
both of which are important in slowing the progress of shock.
The following first aid should be given for crush injuries as
soon as other conditions have been stabilized and while waiting for the ambulance:

- do whatever is possible to minimize pain, but move the
  person as little as possible;

- apply ice bags to the injured part; do not apply direct
  heat;

- treat for shock.

Bleeding from the Ears

Bleeding from the ears may be accompanied by a discharge
of straw-coloured fluid. This indicates a fracture of the skull,
which is very serious (*see chap. 8 - Injuries to Bones and
Joints*). Make no attempt to stop the flow of blood or other
fluids. Do not pack the ear with gauze. Arrange for prompt
medical aid and then give first aid as follows:

- apply a cervical collar;

- secure a sterile dressing loosely over the ear;

- lay the casualty down on the injured side, carefully
  supporting the head and neck, with his upper body
  slightly raised;

- if the casualty vomits or if you must leave him, place him in the recovery position on the injured side;

- check breathing and circulation frequently;

- care for shock (*see chap. 7 - Shock*).

⑥

UNCONSCIOUSNESS AND FAINTING

When a person is fully aware of his surroundings, speaks clearly, responds to speech, is in control of his muscular activity, and reacts to pain, he is said to be conscious. Any change in this state, other than for normal sleep, indicates a loss of consciousness.

Loss of consciousness is a complication of many illnesses and injuries. Head injuries, asphyxia, poisoning, shock and heart attack are some of the conditions which result in unconsciousness. Unconsciousness is dangerous because the person may be unable to swallow, cough or gag. This could cause suffocation as the tongue or fluids block the airway. Prompt and correct first aid to care for the unconscious casualty's airway could well save his life.

LEVELS OF CONSCIOUSNESS

Levels of consciousness *(or degree of unconsciousness)* can be assessed by the person's ability to **open his eyes**, to **speak, to move his hands** or to **respond to pain**.

* a **conscious person** can open his eyes, speak clearly and move his hands to grasp your fingers when asked to do so and will speak out or show, by facial expressions, that he is experiencing pain.

* a **semiconscious person** may open his eyes when spoken to or when experiencing pain. Speech may be confused and not understandable. He may move his extremities but will probably not have a strong grasp or any other effective muscular function.

- an **unconscious person** will not open his eyes, will be unable to speak, will not be able to grasp your hand and will not show much reaction to pain.

The degree of unconsciousness may change as his condition improves or becomes worse. This can be assessed by changes in the degree of response in eye movement, speech, hand movement and reaction to pain. These changes should be described in your notes with a record of the time of each change.

RECOVERY POSITION

An unconscious, breathing person should be placed in the recovery position whenever possible. If he is left on his back, his tongue may fall to the back of the throat to obstruct the airway and he may stop breathing.

If his injuries prevent the use of the recovery position, and other casualties need your attention, have a bystander watch him constantly in case breathing stops.

To move a person from his back to the recovery position:

- kneel at the casualty's waist close to the body and bring the leg on the opposite side toward you, crossing the legs at the ankles.

- tuck the arm nearest you along the side. Bring the other arm across the chest.

Fig. 6-1(a). Cross the legs at the ankles.

- keeping your knees close to the body, place one hand under the head and neck for support, and grip the clothing or belt at the hip on the side away from you.

Fig. 6-1(b). Roll the casualty toward you.

Fig. 6-1(c). Bend the knee.

- roll the person toward you in one smooth, but firm motion. Protect the head and neck during the roll and bring the chest and abdomen to rest on your thighs.

- move back, bending the casualty's knee toward you to prevent the body from rolling forward.

- gently move the head back so that the neck is in an extended position. This helps to keep the airway open.

Fig. 6-1(d). The recovery position.

- bend the upper arm at the elbow to support the weight of the chest. Position the casualty's other arm comfortably along his back to prevent him from rolling backward.

CARE OF THE UNCONSCIOUS CASUALTY

As soon as the casualty is out of danger of further injury from hazards in the area, the immediate objective is to ensure that breathing is maintained or restored. Quickly assess the neck for injuries so that the correct airway opening technique can be applied *(see chap. 3 - Artificial Respiration)*.

Once the airway has been opened and breathing has been restored, the unconscious casualty can be assessed for other injuries, particularly those that might have caused his loss of consciousness. If there are obvious injuries about the face and jaw, check the mouth for knocked-out teeth; remove these to prevent them from being inhaled into the casualty's lungs or swallowed and care for them as amputated tissue (see *chap. 5 - Wounds and Bleeding*).

MEDICAL ALERT INFORMATION

Persons with medical problems that require specific treatment often wear or carry medical information on a bracelet, neck pendant or pocket card. These medical alert devices state the medical condition and may indicate the treatment required. When examining an unconscious casualty, look for such medical information. It may assist in quicker assessment or warn of allergies or health problems that make certain first aid or medical procedures dangerous. Advise medical and ambulance personnel of such information.

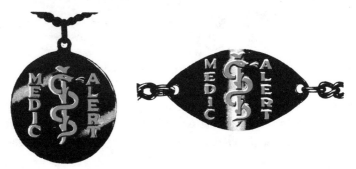

Fig. 6-2. Medic-Alert emblems.

While waiting for transportation to medical aid or on the way to a medical facility, continue first aid to an unconscious casualty as follows:

• monitor breathing closely and be prepared to give artificial respiration if breathing stops.

- reassess the level of consciousness and make a note of any changes, including the times at which these occurred.

- check carefully for neck and back injuries, and place the casualty in the recovery position if his injuries permit.

- care for shock (see *chap. 7 - Shock*).

- give nothing by mouth.

- do not leave unattended except in extreme emergencies. If you must leave to summon help, ensure that the casualty is in the recovery position.

A person who regains consciousness and is not transferred immediately to medical aid should be handed over to the care of responsible people and be advised to see a physician as soon as possible.

FAINTING

Fainting is caused by a temporary shortage of oxygen to the brain. A person who faints will be unconscious, even if only for a few moments. The aim of first aid for fainting is to increase the flow of oxygenated blood to the brain.

Common causes of fainting are:

- long periods of standing or sitting in one position, fatigue, hunger or lack of fresh air;

- emotional stress, such as fear, anxiety or the sight of blood;

- illness, injury or severe pain.

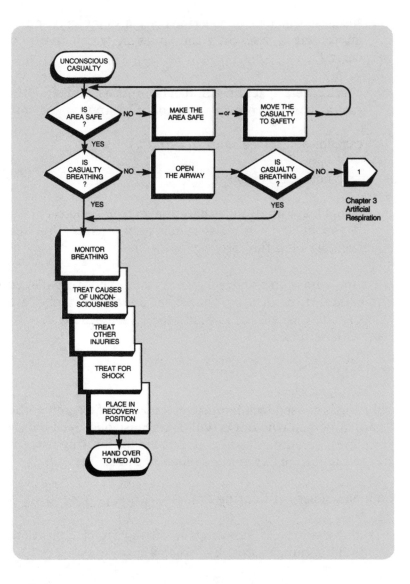

Fig. 6-3. Care of the unconscious person.

There may be some warning of an **impending faint**. The person may feel unsteady *(dizzy)*, become pale and start to perspire. Take the following preventive measures for an impending faint:

- seat the person with his head lowered, or lay him down and raise his feet 15 to 30 cm *(6-12 inches)* above the level of his head;

- ensure a supply of fresh air;

- loosen tight clothing at the neck, chest and waist.

When a person has fainted, you should:

- ensure that his airway is open and that he is breathing;

- loosen tight clothing at the neck, chest and waist;

- place him in the recovery position;

- ensure a supply of fresh air;

- make the person comfortable as consciousness returns and recommend that he remain lying down for 10 to 15 minutes.

If recovery from a faint is not rapid and complete, the person should receive medical attention.

Notes

SHOCK

Shock is a condition of inadequate circulation to the body tissues. It can deprive the brain and other vital organs of oxygen that can lead to unconsciousness and death. Shock may be due to the loss of blood or other body fluids, as in severe bleeding and burns. It may also be the result of fright, pain, nerve injury, heart attack or chemical reaction. *Some degree of shock accompanies every injury and illness.* Shock can be fatal if it is not prevented from worsening.

SIGNS AND SYMPTOMS

The signs and symptoms of shock may develop slowly or rapidly. They are progressive; they become more severe as shock develops. Shock may be recognized by any of the following signs and symptoms:

- restlessness and anxiety *(usually the first sign)*;

- pale or blue-grey colour of the skin, especially earlobes, lips, nostrils and fingernail beds;

- cold, clammy skin and profuse sweating;

- weak and rapid pulse;

- shallow and rapid breathing; gasping for air in later stages;

- thirst;

- nausea and vomiting;

- a decreasing level of consciousness, gradually resulting in total unconsciousness.

FIRST AID

Recognize the conditions that can lead to shock so that first aid can be started early and severe shock prevented. Most major injuries may lead to severe shock, particularly injuries of the abdomen, chest, multiple fractures and fractures of the thighbone. When signs and symptoms of shock are recognized, there must be no delay in getting the casualty to medical aid. Until medical aid is available:

- care for the obvious causes of shock;

- reassure the casualty; tell him what you are doing and why;

- handle the casualty gently to avoid causing pain;

- loosen tight clothing around the neck, chest and waist;

- keep the casualty warm with clothing, blankets, etc., but do not use hot water bottles;

- wipe his face, moisten his lips and comfort him.

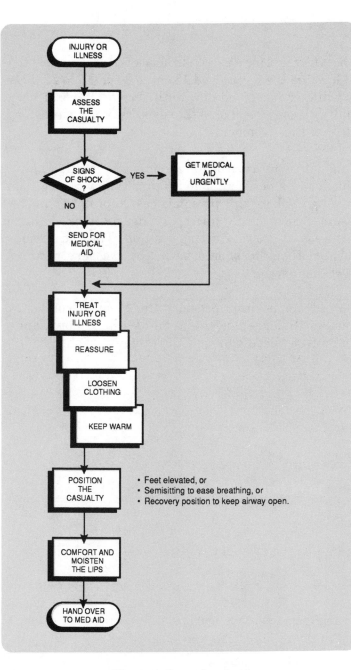

Fig. 7-1. Care for shock.

The Shock Position

The best position for a person in shock is on his back with the head low and the feet raised 15 cm to 30 cm *(6 to 12 inches)*. This will increase blood flow to the brain. Raise either the casualty's legs and feet or, if the casualty is on a stretcher, lift the foot of the stretcher.

The casualty's injuries or illness may not permit you to use the ideal shock position. Pelvic injuries may be aggravated by raising the legs; this person is best kept flat on his back. A casualty with chest injuries, or a heart attack victim may breathe easier in a semisitting position. The unconscious or nauseated casualty should be in the recovery position to protect his airway.

Use whatever position provides the greatest comfort, but remember that keeping the casualty's head down and his legs and feet raised will slow the progress of shock.

8

INJURIES TO BONES
AND JOINTS

Injuries to bones and joints fall into three categories; fractures, dislocations and sprains. These injuries may occur one at a time or in combination. A limb that is violently wrenched may have a sprained or dislocated joint with bone fractures.

PREVENTION

Simple safety precautions and the proper use of safety equipment can prevent most accidents that cause injuries to bones and joints. Take the following precautions:

- practise good housekeeping at home and at work. Keep work areas clean. Wipe up liquids and grease at once. Use nonskid wax on floors at all times.

- remove throw rugs from the top and bottom of stairways and avoid their use elsewhere unless you use nonskid underpads.

- anchor ladders safely at the top and bottom. Avoid overreaching when working from a ladder.

- use a safety belt and line when working at dangerous heights.

- use protective equipment such as helmets, pads, guards and gloves for dangerous work or sports activities.

- use correct body mechanics to lift or move heavy objects (see *chap. 14 - Rescue and Transportation).*

- operate motor vehicles carefully, with the safety of yourself and others in mind at all times.

FRACTURES

A fracture is any break or crack in a bone. The most important factor in assessing fractures is the condition of the surrounding tissue:

- **closed fractures** are those over which the surrounding skin is unbroken;

- **open fractures** are those over which the skin is broken; bone ends may protrude.

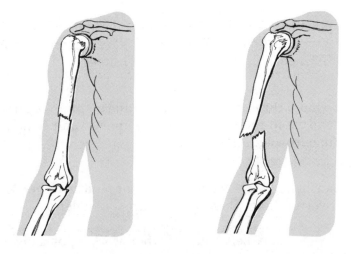

Fig. 8-1. Closed and open fractures.

Closed fractures cause internal bleeding, but will not become contaminated if the skin remains unbroken. The wound associated with an open fracture causes external bleeding and permits germs to enter.

Fractures are also described as **complicated** when broken bones have injured other tissue such as nerves, blood vessels or internal organs.

SIGNS AND SYMPTOMS

Fractures can be recognized by the presence of some or all of the following signs and symptoms:

- **pain** at the injury site, made worse by movement;

- **loss of function** — the inability to use the limb;

- **swelling** and **discolouration**, which can be detecte by comparing the size and colour of the injured limb with the one that is not injured;

- **deformity** and **irregularity** — the abnormal position of the limb or irregular line of the bone under the skin;

- **tenderness** — pain caused by touching the injury;

- **shock** that increases with the severity of the injury;

- **unnatural movement** as the limb bends or moves at the injury site;

- **crepitus** — the grating noise that may be heard as the broken ends of bones rub together. *Never move broken bones in an attempt to create this sound.*

Fractures of the chest, multiple fractures and fractures of long bones, such as the thighbone may cause shock to be severe.

FIRST AID FOR FRACTURES - GENERAL RULES

The objectives of first aid for fractures and other bone injuries are to prevent further damage and to reduce pain. *Do only what is needed to achieve these aims.* Do not put the casualty through the discomfort of splinting if medical aid is readily available. With this in mind, give only the first aid that is needed:

• give first aid where the casualty is found. If there is danger in the immediate surroundings, provide temporary support for the fracture while moving the casualty to safety.

• slowly and steadily realign a fractured limb with gentle traction to a position of natural alignment and maintain this position with traction and support. This may be all that is needed if medical aid is readily available.

• dress wounds to stop bleeding and to prevent further contamination of an open fracture. Protect any protruding bone ends with a ring pad over the dressings, but do not force a bone end back into the wound.

• immobilize the fracture by securing the limb to a padded splint or to a healthy limb with bandages if the casualty must be transported to medical aid.

• raise and support an injured limb after immobilization to reduce bleeding and swelling.

• monitor circulation to the injured limb below the fracture to ensure that bandages are not too tight.

MONITORING CIRCULATION

Circulation to the fingers and toes can be monitored by checking the colour of the fingernails or toenails and by assessing the temperature of the injured limb below the fracture. Press on a fingernail or toenail until its colour changes from pink to white. If circulation to the limb is good, the colour should return as soon as the pressure is released. If the nail remains white or bluish or takes a long time to return to a healthy colour, circulation to the area is probably restricted. Similarly, if the fingers or toes of the injured limb are colder than those of the other limb, impaired circulation should be suspected. If circulation cannot be restored by gently adjusting the limb or loosening bandages, medical aid is needed urgently.

TRACTION

When immobilizing limb fractures steady and support the limb throughout the procedure. Unless the injury is at a joint, apply gentle traction to the limb. To apply traction, draw gently and steadily on the end of the limb below the fracture, using only enough tension to relieve pain and to realign the limb.

Fig. 8-2. Applying traction to the lower limb.

If pain is increased, ease the tension. Once traction is applied it must be maintained steadily until the fracture is immobilized. Advise medical authorities either with a written note or by telling them that traction has been applied to a fractured limb.

Do not use traction on a joint injury because it may cause further damage to nerves and major blood vessels that pass close to the joint. Steady and support such injuries in the position of greatest comfort.

SPLINTS

When a casualty with a fracture must be transported to medical aid or if there is a long delay in obtaining medical aid, splint the fracture to prevent further movement of the broken bones. Any material that is rigid, long enough to extend beyond the joints above and below the fracture, and wide enough to provide comfort can be used as a splint. Some commercial splints are so compact and light that they can be carried in first aid kits. Splints can be improvised from pieces of board, cardboard, magazines, a walking stick or a hockey stick. If these are not available, uninjured parts of the body, such as a lower limb or the chest can be used as a splint.

PADDING AND BANDAGES

When splinting a fracture, place padding between the injured limb and the splint. Put extra padding at the natural hollows and pad the ends of the splint. Use soft padding between parts of the body that are to be bandaged together to reduce friction and discomfort.

Use broad bandages whenever possible to secure splints to a limb, but do not let the bandages overlap the fracture site. Narrow bandages may have to be used on short limbs and on children. Tie the knots on the uninjured side so that the broadest part of the bandage is on the injured limb, or tie bandages on the splint itself. If both lower limbs are injured, tie bandages off midway between the legs.

SPLINTING FRACTURES

The application of splints and bandages varies slightly from one part of the body to another, but the general rules of first aid for fractures apply in all cases and should be kept in mind when immobilizing the following fractures.

Collarbone

Fracture of the collarbone is commonly caused by a fall on the outstretched hand, but it may also be caused by a blow or other direct force. The injured person usually supports the arm at the elbow and inclines the head toward the injured side to relieve pain. Muscles attached to the bone will provide some support if there is no movement. The aims of first aid for a fractured collarbone are to give further support and to immobilize the arm and shoulder as follows:

- support the arm on the injured side in a St. John tubular sling to transfer its weight to the opposite side;

- secure the supported arm to the body in the position that the casualty finds most comfortable. Use a narrow

Fig. 8-3.
Immobilizing a
fractured
collarbone.

bandage, starting with the centre at the elbow and tying off on the opposite side of the body.

Upper Arm

The upper arm may be fractured anywhere along its length or at either end where it forms the joints of the shoulder and the elbow. If the injury is near a joint, take special precautions to avoid damage to nerves and major blood vessels. If the injury is along the length of the bone and the elbow joint can be bent, immobilize the upper arm as follows:

- position the forearm across the chest;

- support the forearm in an arm sling;

- place soft padding between the chest and the full length of the upper arm;

- secure the upper arm to the chest by a bandage above and one below the fracture;

Fig. 8-4. Immobilizing a fractured upper arm.

- check circulation to the fingers frequently and reposition the arm or loosen bandages if circulation is impaired.

Lower Arm

Either one or both of the two bones of the lower arm *(forearm)* may be broken where they join with the upper arm to form the elbow, along their lengths or where they join with the bones of the wrist to form the wrist joint. If the fracture is near the elbow or wrist, immobilize it as a joint injury. Immobilize fractures along the length of the bones as follows:

• steady and support the lower arm in the most comfortable position, usually across the chest.

• apply a padded splint along the palm side of the arm from the elbow to the base of the fingers. Secure it with narrow bandages above and below the fracture.

• support the forearm across the chest, slightly elevated, and apply an arm sling.

Fig. 8-5. Immobilizing a fracture of the forearm.

• monitor circulation to the fingers.

Hand and Fingers

Fractures of the hand and fingers or a crushed hand are best supported by resting the hand on a pillow in the most comfortable position. If the casualty must be transported to medical aid, immobilize the hand as follows:

- place a roll of loose gauze or other soft material in the palm and under the fingers to maintain the position of function with the fingers slightly curled;

- place the hand, palm side down, on a well-padded splint that extends from the fingertips to the elbow;

- if the fingers are crushed, place nonstick dressings between the fingers;

- secure the hand gently to the splint with broad bandages or with a roller bandage, starting from the fingertips and working to the upper end of the splint;

- support the hand in a slightly elevated position in an arm sling.

Fig. 8-6. Immobilizing a fractured hand.

Thighbone

Fractures of the thighbone are always serious because of the loss of blood into the tissues and the possibility of shock. Fractures may occur at the upper end of the femur at the hip joint, along the length of the bone or at the knee joint *(see Joint Injuries for fractures involving the knee).* Fractures of the femur may be recognized by the fact that one leg is shorter and by the unnatural outward turn of the foot.

If medical aid is readily available, support the entire leg with gentle but firm traction to keep the limb in proper body alignment with the toes and kneecap pointed upward. Maintain traction and support until medical aid arrives. Do whatever you can to slow the progress of shock.

If the casualty must be moved, immobilize the fracture with a splint long enough to extend from the armpit to below the foot. Pad the splint well, especially at its upper end and at the natural hollows of the body. Provide sufficient padding to be placed between the legs.

Have someone maintain traction and support while you position seven bandages so that both legs will be secured and so that the knots will be tied over the splint. Slide the bandages under the body at the natural hollows of the back, knees and ankles, using a small flat stick. Ease them up or down into the desired position as follows:

- one broad bandage at the chest just below the armpits;

- one broad bandage at the pelvis in line with the hip joint;

- two broad or narrow bandages, depending on the size of the casualty, one above and one below the fracture;

- one broad bandage midway between the knees and ankles;

- one broad bandage at the knees;

- one narrow or broad bandage at the ankles.

When all the bandages are in position, place padding between the legs and place the padded splint on the outside of the body along the injured side. Secure the body and legs to the splint by tying off the bandages in the following order:

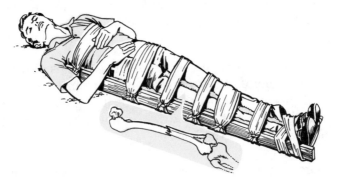

Fig. 8-7. Splinting a fractured thighbone.

* chest;

* pelvis;

* ankles and feet in a figure-8;

* thighs, above and below the fracture;

* knees;

* lower legs.

Omit any bandage that will put pressure on the fracture or give the casualty added discomfort.

If the casualty must be moved and a long splint is not available, some degree of immobilization can be achieved by using the good leg as a splint. Have someone maintain traction and support while five bandages are put in position: one above and one below the fracture; one at the knees; one at the lower legs; and one under the ankles.

Place padding between the legs (*a rolled blanket is ideal*) and move the good leg in against the padding. Secure the two legs together in the following order:

- ankles and feet in a figure-8. Maintain traction on the injured leg by locking the edge of the shoe on the injured side under the edge of the shoe on the uninjured side.

- thighs, above and below the fracture.

- knees.

- lower legs.

Lower Leg

Fractures of the lower leg may involve one or both bones. If the tibia *(the larger bone)* is fractured, the fibula *(the smaller bone)* may be fractured as well. If fractures do not involve the knee joint or the ankle, apply gentle traction to support and realign the limb and maintain this support until the casualty is under medical care or the limb is immobilized. Splinting is needed if medical aid is delayed or if the casualty must be moved to medical care. Splints, secured to either side of the injured leg, make it easier to transport the casualty in a car or other improvised transportation.

Two-Splint Method. Prepare two splints long enough to extend the full length of the leg and just beyond the foot. Use the natural hollows at the knee and ankle to position five bandages under the injured leg as follows:

- one broad bandage at the upper thigh;

- one narrow bandage at a point above the fracture site;

- one broad bandage at the knee;

- one narrow bandage at a point below the fracture site;

- one broad bandage at the ankle.

Place any additional padding required at the natural hollows of the leg at the knee and ankle and position the splints, one on either side of the leg, ready to be secured by the five bandages. Tie the bandages over the splints in the following order:

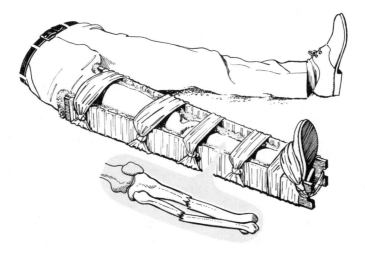

Fig. 8-8. Immobilizing a fracture of the lower leg.

- at the thigh;

- at the ankle to include the splints and foot;

- at the knee;

- above the fracture;

- below the fracture.

Body- Splint Method. If commercial or improvised splints are not available and the casualty must be moved, a fracture of the lower leg can be immobilized by using the good leg as a natural splint.

While the injured limb is steadied and supported with gentle traction, position bandages under both limbs. Place padding along the inside of the injured limb to fill the hollows and to protect the ankles and knees. Bring the uninjured limb next to the injured one. Lock the edge of the shoe on the injured side under the edge of the shoe on the uninjured side to maintain traction. Secure the two legs together, tying the bandages on the uninjured side or over the centre padding, in the following sequence:

- a narrow or broad bandage at the ankles in a figure-8;

- a broad bandage at the thighs;

- a broad bandage around the knees;

- a narrow bandage above the fracture site; and

- a narrow bandage below the fracture site.

Ankle and Foot

Loosen footwear in all injuries of the ankle or foot in which fractures are suspected. This is to avoid constriction of the foot as swelling occurs and to permit a check of the foot for wounds.

If wounds are present, gently remove footwear, cutting it away if necessary, so that dressings and bandages can be applied. If there are no wounds, leave the footwear in place to serve as a splint for immobilization.

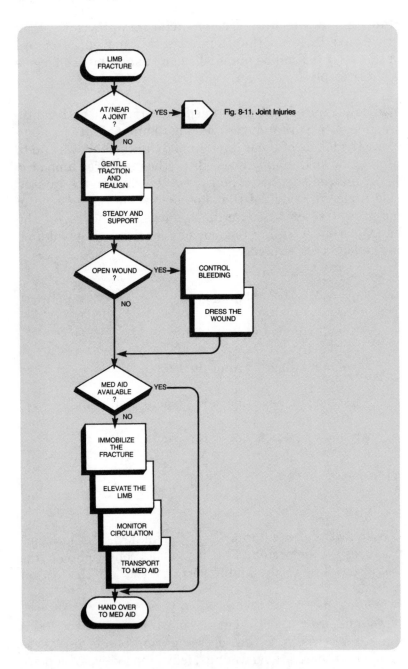

Fig. 8-9. Care of a fractured limb.

Immobilize the foot in a pillow or blanket secured with bandages. Raise the foot and support it in a comfortable position— usually 15 cm to 30 cm. *(6-12 inches).* Transport to medical aid on a stretcher.

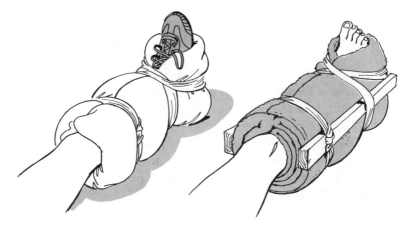

Fig. 8-10. Immobilizing the ankle and foot.

JOINT INJURIES

A **dislocation** occurs when the bones are forced out of position and proper contact with each other. Supporting tissues are stretched or torn and there may be a fracture near the joint or a break in the bone surfaces at the joint. A joint may be **sprained** when the bones are moved beyond their normal limits and the surrounding tissues are stretched or torn.

Major blood vessels and nerves pass around the bones at joints, particularly the joints at the shoulder, elbow, hip and knee. Damage to these blood vessels can cut off circulation to the extremity and nerve damage can cause permanent injury. Whenever there are bone injuries, try to determine if a joint is involved. If so, take extra care to prevent movement of the joint, especially if the movement causes pain. Always consider the possibility that a joint injury may include a fracture.

Cold Application. Pain and swelling that accompanies all joint injuries can be relieved and controlled by the use of cold. Commercially prepared chemical cold packs with printed instructions for activating the chemicals are available for first aid kits. An ice pack can be prepared by filling a rubber or plastic bag two-thirds full of crushed ice, expelling excess air from the bag and sealing the opening to make it water-tight. Wrap cold packs or ice packs in a towel if they are to be applied to the bare skin.   Apply ice or cold packs — 15 minutes on, 15 minutes off. ***Do not apply these packs directly to bare skin — the cold can cause tissue damage.*** If ice is not available, cold compresses can be made by soaking a towel in cold water, wringing out the excess water and wrapping the towel around the affected part. Cold water can be added to the compress from time to time or it can be replaced with a fresh one.

DISLOCATIONS

Dislocations are painful and will become swollen and discoloured. The joint usually appears deformed where the bones are out of position and the casualty is unable to move the joint. Any movement will cause severe pain and should be avoided. Make no attempt to return bones to their normal position.

Give first aid for dislocations as follows:

*   steady and support the injured limb in the position that gives the most comfort. Use pillows, cushions or blan-

kets to pad the injured limb in place and secure with bandages or a sling *(see chap. 5 - Wounds and Bleeding)*.

• monitor circulation closely. If circulation is impaired, transport to medical aid urgently.

• apply ice packs to the joint (15 minutes on, 15 minutes off) to help relieve pain and control swelling.

• transport to medical aid.

SPRAINS

Sprains can be recognized by pain, swelling, bruise-discolouration and inability to use the limb, although it may be possible for the casualty to bend the joint. Circulation may be impaired and swelling may be severe, but there should not be marked deformity of the joint.

It may be difficult to tell if a joint injury includes a fracture so give first aid for a sprain as if it is fractured as follows:

• apply gentle pressure with bandages *(Compression)* to control swelling;

• immobilize and raise the injured limb *(Elevation)* if possible;

• apply ice packs *(Ice)* (15 minutes on, 15 minutes off) to the joint to reduce pain and to control swelling.

Remember the word ICE to help you in applying basic first aid for a sprain — **I**ce, **C**ompression and **E**levation.

Monitor circulation to the extremity and transport to medical aid.

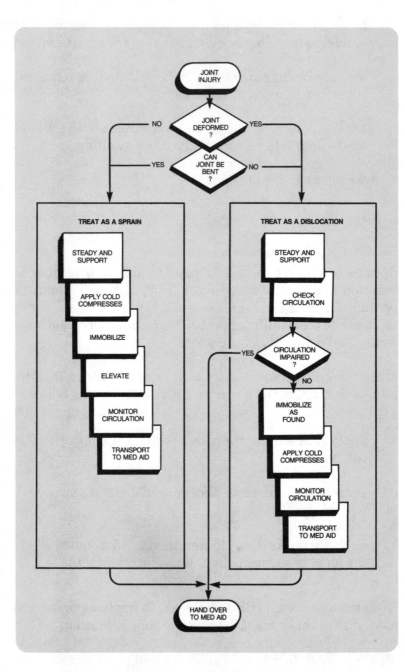

Fig. 8-11. Care of joint injuries.

SPECIAL FRACTURE INJURIES

Crush injuries and fractures of the chest, pelvis, head and spine usually involve other major and vital organs and require special care.

Crush Injuries

A person who has been crushed by heavy equipment or masonry may have multiple fractures and may have extensive injuries to muscles and other tissues with possible rupture of internal organs. This casualty is in grave danger of severe shock caused by the massive crushing of tissues (*see chap. 5 -Wounds and Bleeding*).

Flail Chest

A severe blow or crushing force to the chest often fractures a number of ribs in more than one place. This may cause a segment of the chest wall to move abnormally during breathing. When breathing in, the segment is sucked in and when breathing out, it is blown outward.

This is known as a flail chest and causes painful, ineffective breathing, leading to distress and oxygen lack. Therefore, first aid should aim to reassure the casualty, help him to breathe easier and get him to medical help.

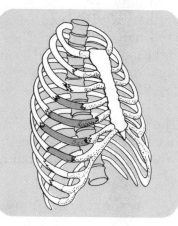

Fig. 8-12. A flail chest.

Stabilize the injured segment by placing the casualty's arm across the injury and securing the arm to the chest with broad bandages. A firm pad or cushion, secured to the chest with tape or bandages, may also be used as a splint. Position the casualty in a semisitting position, inclined toward the injured side, to make breathing easier and to allow the lung on the uninjured side to function more freely.

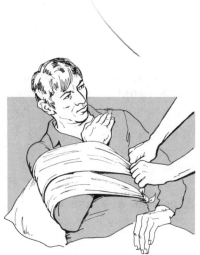

Fig. 8-13. Care for a flail chest.

Fracture of the Pelvis

A fracture of the pelvis is usually caused by a direct crushing force or a fall and may involve injury to the organs of the pelvic area, particularly the bladder and urethra. Persons with such injuries may pass bloody urine or may be unable to urinate. They should be advised to try not to urinate. A casualty with a fractured pelvis may feel pain in the hips and the small of the back. They may be unable to stand or walk. If the pain is increased by movement, the casualty should be kept very still. Watch carefully for signs of shock and get medical aid urgently if these are observed.

The extent of first aid for a fractured pelvis depends on the distance to a medical facility and the smoothness of the trip. When medical aid is readily available:

*   lay the casualty in the most comfortable position, usually on his back with knees straight. If the person wishes to bend his knees, support them with a folded blanket or pillow.

- pad the ankles and secure the feet together with a narrow bandage in a figure-8 if it does not increase discomfort.

- support both sides of the pelvis with padded weights, e.g., sandbags or books.

When medical aid is delayed or if transportation is long or rough:

- place soft padding between the knees and ankles.

- apply a figure-8 bandage around the ankles and feet.

- apply two broad bandages around the pelvis, overlapping by half. The broad parts of the bandages should be on the injured side in line with the hip joint. Tie off gently or fasten with a safety pin on the uninjured side. *If the casualty complains of discomfort, loosen or remove the bandages immediately*. Support both sides of the pelvic area with weights.

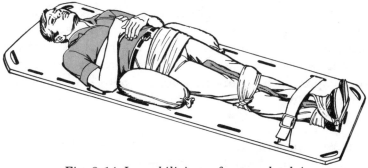

Fig. 8-14. Immobilizing a fractured pelvis.

- apply a broad bandage around the knees.

- place the casualty on a long, padded spine board, using the logroll manoeuvre and transport to medical aid.

Head Injuries

Fractures of the skull are especially dangerous because the force that caused the fracture may also have injured the brain. These injuries can cause bleeding in the skull, which will put pressure on the brain, and result in unconsciousness *(see chap. 6 -Unconsciousness)* and breathing difficulties *(see chap. 3 - Artificial Respiration)*. Pressure on the brain can sometimes be recognized by the unequal size of the pupils of the eyes *(see fig. 13-1)*. First aid for scalp wounds and bleeding from the ears and nose is described in chapter 5 - Wounds and Bleeding.

Anyone who sustains a head injury should receive medical care. A neck fracture should always be suspected in injuries resulting from a blow to the head or a fall from any height. Give first aid to these casualties as if the neck were fractured.

Neck Injuries

The neck may be fractured by a blow to the head, by violent movement backward *(extension)* and forward *(flexion)*, as in a whiplash injury, and by striking the head, as in diving accidents and hockey accidents. The casualty with a neck injury experiences severe pain and, if he is conscious, may complain of loss of feeling or paralysis.

The most important first aid for a suspected neck injury is to steady and support the head and neck in the position found to prevent movement in any direction. This is done, initially, by placing the hands on either side of the casualty's head with the fingers running along the line of the jaw. If the head must be moved to clear the airway, use gentle traction as you move the head. To open the airway, use the jaw thrust without head tilt and, if required, give artificial respiration *(see chap. 3 - Artificial Respiration)*.

Apply a cervical collar to keep the head and neck steady. Such a collar can be improvised with triangular bandages as follows:

• lay out a triangular bandage as a whole cloth on a flat surface.

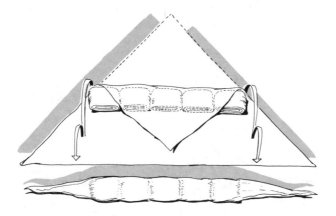

Fig. 8-15. Improvising a cervical collar.

• place soft, bulky material on a line about one third the distance from the **POINT** to the **BASE**. Five folded triangular bandages, several pairs of folded socks, several folded scarves or a piece of a blanket make suitable padding for this purpose.

• fold the **POINT** toward the **BASE** to enclose the line of padding. Roll the padding and bandage toward the **BASE** to form a collar about 8 cm to 10 cm *(3-4 inches)* in diameter with ties on each end to secure it around the neck.

- place the centre of the collar under the casualty's chin and ease the **ENDS** under the neck, using a small thin stick.

- bring the **ENDS** around and tie them off gently under the chin on the wide part of the collar.

Steady and support the head and neck throughout the application of the cervical collar and until such time as the head is immobilized to a spine board.

A casualty found in a sitting position should have his head, neck and upper body immobilized as one unit if he must be moved.

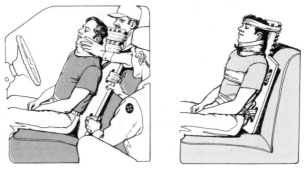

Fig. 8-16. Applying a short spine board.

With the head and neck immobilized in a cervical collar and firmly supported by hand, slide a short spine board or other rigid material behind the casualty with as little movement as possible. Secure the casualty's head and body to the board with narrow and broad bandages, tying off on the edge of the board if possible.

BACK INJURIES

Dislocations and fractures of the spine are serious injuries that can involve the spinal cord and nerves to other parts of the body. Any movement can increase the chances of shock and cause permanent paralysis. First aid for back injuries should *prevent the casualty from moving* and should slow the progress of shock until medical aid arrives *(see chap. 7 - Shock)*.

Do not move a person with a back injury, but if he must be moved, the following are required to minimize the risk of causing further injury:

- a minimum of four, but preferably more bearers.

- a long spine board, prepared or improvised. Make certain that an improvised spine board is strong enough to bear the casualty's weight, wide enough to ensure proper support and narrow enough to clear doors and passageways through which the casualty will be carried.

- padding sufficient to fill the hollows between the thighs and legs, and to fill the spaces along the spine board at the natural hollows at the neck, small of the back, knees and ankles.

- bandages sufficient to immobilize the joints at the hips, knees, legs, ankles and feet, and to secure the casualty to the spine board.

- a suction bulb to clear the casualty's airway during movement. A rubber syringe or a plastic kitchen baster may be used.

Immobilization of a Spinal Injury

Prevent the casualty's spine from twisting or turning during immobilization by having one rescuer hold the head and neck and another hold the feet and ankles. These two

rescuers should exert gentle traction and maintain it throughout immobilization. Then proceed as follows:

* apply a cervical collar;

* position broad bandages under the body at the hip joint,
  at the knees and under the lower legs, and a narrow
  bandage under the ankles. Slide the bandages under
  the natural hollows of the body with a small flat stick;
  then ease them into position so that they can be tied off
  along the centre line of the body.

* place padding between the legs to fill the hollows and to
  protect the knees and ankles.

* tie the bandages firmly to prevent movement of the
  joints. Secure the ankles and feet with a figure-8 while
  the two rescuers maintain body traction.

* place the casualty's forearms across the chest and
  secure them gently with a bandage. Explain to the
  casualty that this is to prevent them from falling to the
  sides and causing body movement.

THE LOGROLL MANOEUVRE

When the casualty is immobilized, place the spine board
alongside the casualty with padding and straps in position.
The padding should correspond to the natural hollows of the
body at the neck, the small of the back, the knees and the
ankles. The straps should be in position to secure the
casualty to the board. Take care that padding will not put
pressure on the fracture site. Position and instruct the
rescue team as follows:

* instruct the two rescuers at the head and feet to maintain body traction throughout the procedure and to
  rotate the head and feet in unison with the roll of the

body to prevent twisting of the head and spine. Caution the rescuer at the head to be especially careful not to allow the head to bend forward.

• tell one or more rescuers to take positions along the casualty's side away from the spine board at the hips and lower legs. They should reach over the casualty to grasp clothing to enable them to roll the casualty toward them onto his side when directed to do so.

• have one rescuer control the spine board and move it into position when the casualty is rolled over onto his side. He should make the final padding adjustment before the casualty is rolled back onto the board and help to slide the casualty over the centre of the board.

• if you are the First Aider, take the position at the shoulders so that you can control the rescue team and pay particular attention to the neck and upper back during the manoeuvre.

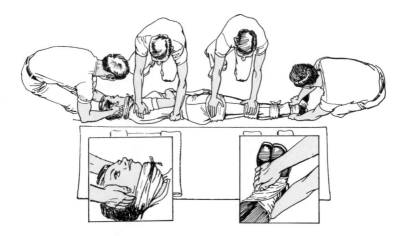

Fig. 8-17. Logroll unto a prepared spine board.

When you are satisfied that everyone is in position and ready, direct the team to roll the casualty gently onto his side. Ensure that the spine board and padding are in proper position and direct the bearers to roll the casualty back onto the board.

Cover the casualty with a blanket and secure him to the board with bandages or straps before the board is carried. Monitor breathing and transport to medical care as smoothly as possible.

9

EYE INJURIES

Sight, that most important of all the senses, depends on one of the most delicate and sensitive organs of the body, the eye. It takes so little to impair eyesight that extra care should be taken to protect the eyes from hazards. However, if the eyes are endangered, immediate and correct first aid may prevent impairment of vision or the complete loss of eyesight.

PREVENTION

Make a determined effort to protect the eyes:

- with glasses and goggles when grinding, drilling, cutting metals or using chisels.

- by wearing recommended safety goggles for sports with fast moving targets such as racquet ball, squash, etc.

- from chemical splashes, corrosive powders, aerosol sprays and fumes. Keep chemicals off high shelves and take care when handling large containers of liquid chemicals to avoid splashes. Read WHMIS *(Workplace Hazardous Materials Information System)* labels and MSDS *(Material Safety Data Sheets)* to know the correct eye protection for the chemical in use.

- from arc welding flash and other bright lights. Use dark goggles or eye shields and avoid looking at direct sunlight. The sun's reflection from snow can cause snowblindness if dark glasses are not worn.

PARTICLES IN THE EYE

Loose eyelashes, particles of sand and fragments of glass or metal may lodge on the eyeball causing pain. The eye will become inflamed, giving it a red appearance. Tears help to loosen and wash away such particles. Do not attempt to remove any particle from the eye when it is embedded in or adhered to the eyeball. In these cases:

- warn the person not to rub the eye. This will cause more pain and irritation.

- wash your hands before starting first aid.

- cover the injured eye with an eye or gauze pad large enough to extend beyond the eye. Secure it lightly in position with adhesive strips.

- transport the casualty to medical aid.

If the particle can be seen and if it is not stuck to the eyeball, remove it with a moist corner of a facial tissue or corner of a moist clean cloth.

If the particle is under the upper lid, the person can sometimes remove it by pulling the upper lid down over the lower lid. The lashes of the lower lid act as a brush and may dislodge and remove the particle.

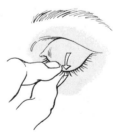

Fig. 9-1. Removal of a particle from the upper eyelid.

EXAMINATION OF
THE UPPER EYELID

It may be necessary to examine the inner surface of the upper eyelid to locate and remove a particle. To examine the eyelid:

- seat the person facing a light, stand behind and to the side, tilt the head back, and ask the person to look down.

  - place an applicator stick or a matchstick at the base of the upper lid, and press the lid slightly backwards.

  - gently grasp the upper eyelashes between the thumb and index finger. Draw the lid away from the eye, up and over the applicator stick, and roll the applicator back. This will turn the eyelid outward and expose the underside.

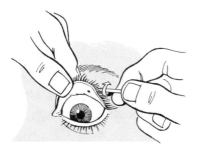

Fig. 9-2. Turning back the upper eyelid.

- remove the particle with the moist corner of a facial tissue or clean cloth.

- gently replace the upper eyelid in its proper position.

- obtain medical aid if pain persists.

EXAMINATION OF
THE LOWER EYELID

To expose the inside of the lower eyelid for examination, and to remove a particle, proceed as follows:

- seat the person facing a light;

- stand in front and gently draw the lower eyelid downwards and away from the eyeball while the person rolls the eye upward.

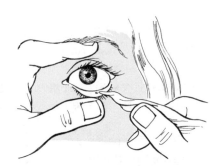

Fig. 9-3. Removal of a particle from the lower eyelid.

This may expose the particle, and it can be wiped away with the moist corner of a facial tissue or clean cloth.

EXAMINATION OF THE EYEBALL

Particles on the eyeball can sometimes be difficult to see in direct light. A light shone across the surface of the eyeball will sometimes cast a shadow of the particle, showing its location.

If a loose particle is located in this way and it is not on the coloured part of the eye, remove it with the moist corner of a clean tissue or cloth.

If the light fails to locate a particle in the eye, do not persist. Further attempts to remove the object may be unsuccessful and can aggravate the injury. Cover the injured eye and take the person to medical aid.

EMBEDDED OBJECTS

Workers should be on the alert to the possibility of eye injury by flying debris. Sudden discomfort in the eye while hammering or sawing without safety glasses should suggest penetration by a metallic or other object, even if the pain seems to subside rapidly.

Large particles may penetrate or become embedded in the eyeball or in the tissue surrounding the eye. Do not attempt to remove these embedded objects:

- lay the casualty down and support the head to reduce movement;

- gently place dressings around the object;

Fig. 9-4. Protecting an object embedded in the eye.

- cover the eye with a paper cup or cone to prevent any pressure on the object;

- secure the cup and dressings in place with tape. A roller bandage may be necessary to help hold bulky dressings in place;

- ensure that no pressure is applied to the embedded object and the eye;

- place the casualty on a stretcher and immobilize the head with weights, books, blocks etc. on either side of the head. This will prevent side to side movement;

- transport the casualty to medical aid.

LACERATIONS AND CONTUSIONS

Lacerations about the eye will bleed profusely, but this may not be serious. The real danger is that the eyeball may have been lacerated. Contusions around the eye are usually the result of a blow by a blunt object. The skin may not be broken, but there may be injury to the underlying bone or to the eyeball. Vision may be affected, and the eye may appear "bloodshot". These injuries may be serious and there is grave danger that eyesight will be impaired if the eyeball has been damaged. Never apply pressure to the eyeball.

Give first aid for these injuries as follows:

• have the person lie down and support the head;

• cover the injured eye with an eye or gauze pad secured lightly with a bandage or adhesive strips;

• immobilize the head to prevent side-to-side movement;

• transport the casualty to medical aid on a stretcher with a minimum of jostling.

CHEMICAL BURNS

Chemicals in the eyes should be removed immediately to reduce eye damage. Quickly brush out dry chemicals, such as lime, before flushing the eyes with water for 10 to 15 minutes. Quickly flush liquid chemicals out of the injured

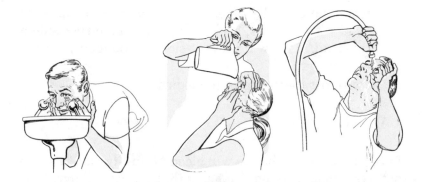

Fig. 9-5. Emergency eye washes.

eye, keeping it open with the fingers so that the chemical will be diluted and washed away.

If running water is not available, sit or lay the person down with the head tilted back and toward the injured side. Cover the uninjured eye and flush the chemical out of the other eye with tepid or cool water. Gently hold the eyelids apart so that the substance will be flushed out.

After flushing, cover the injured eye with dressings and arrange for immediate medical aid. If both eyes are injured, cover the eye that is more seriously injured. If the casualty is more comfortable with both eyes covered, cover both eyes.

It is recommended to only cover the more seriously injured eye to avoid the psychological stress that the casualty suffers when blinded by covering both eyes. If both eyes must be covered due to serious injury in both eyes (e.g. intense light burn from arc welding, *see below*) reassure the casualty often by explaining what is being done.

BURNS FROM INTENSE LIGHT

Direct or reflected sunlight, arc welder's flash, infrared rays or laser beams can injure the light-sensitive portions of the eye (e.g. snowblindness). These injuries may not be painful at first, but may become very painful 3 to 5 hours after exposure. Permanent damage to vision may result.

If the casualty complains of a burning sensation in the eyes caused by an earlier exposure to bright light, cover both eyes with thick, moist pads and tape them in place to exclude light and to cool the eyes. Reassure the casualty as he is now blinded by the pads and bandages. Transport the casualty to medical aid.

Notes

10

BURNS

A burn is any damage to the skin or other tissues caused by dry or moist heat, chemical action, electrical energy or radiation. The majority of injuries from burns occur in the home, and the victims are most often the elderly and the very young.

PREVENTION

Almost all burn injuries can be avoided by an awareness of the dangers in the home and in the workplace and by using the following simple safety precautions.

Protect children from burns by:

- setting water tank thermostats not higher than 54°C *(130°F)*;

- preparing a child's bath with cold water, and then adding hot water to reach the desired temperature;

- preventing children from chewing on electric cords, which can result in severe burns of the mouth;

- safeguarding children from sunburn with protective clothing and sunscreen lotions;

- keeping containers of hot liquids out of the reach of children.

Protect the elderly from burns by:

• ensuring that their clothing is not flammable;

• guarding them from stoves and open flames when they are wearing loose clothing, nightgowns, etc.;

• supervising their use of stoves, fires and smoking materials — matches, lighters, cigarettes, cigars and pipes.

Protect other household members from burns by:

• ensuring that pot handles are turned toward the back of the stove;

• lifting pot lids away from you to control steam;

• using hand protection when lifting pots from the stove;

• developing and practising a fire escape plan and ensuring that everyone is familiar with it, including babysitters.

Protect the home from fires by:

• having your home inspected by the fire department and heeding their advice on fireproofing;

• testing smoke alarms periodically to ensure that they are working properly;

• keeping fire department telephone numbers posted near the telephone and ensuring that family members know the location of the nearest fire alarm call box;

- keeping fire extinguishers ready and training family members in their use;

- not using gasoline or other flammables as cleaning agents;

- storing flammables, oily rags, etc. in sealed cans away from heat sources;

- storing propane tanks outside the house in a well-ventilated place.

TYPES OF BURNS

The characteristics of most burns depend, to some degree, on their causes:

- **dry heat burns**, such as those caused by fire or contact with hot objects, may involve a large area of the body and may have areas of deep injury.

- **moist heat burns**, caused by steam or hot liquids, are usually superficial, but they may be very serious if the face, genitals or large areas of the body are involved.

- **chemical burns**, such as those from sulphuric acid, caustic soda or other corrosive chemicals, quickly cause skin damage that continues as long as the chemical is in contact with the skin. These injuries are especially dangerous if chemicals are taken into the mouth, because they may injure the airway and interfere with breathing.

- **electric burns**, caused by the passage of electric current through the body, result in deep injuries at the point of entry and at the point of exit. Electric burns are often accompanied by asphyxia and by cardiac arrest *(see chap. 3 - Artificial Respiration)*. There may also be fractures and dislocations from the violent muscular contraction due to the electric shock.

- **radiation burns**, most commonly caused by overexposure to the sun, cover a large area of the body and are usually very painful. They may cause blistering and swelling.

The seriousness of a burn depends mainly on its depth and the size of the burned area. Other conditions, such as the age of the casualty, his physical condition and the location of the burn on the body, also affect the degree of danger.

Burns are classified by depth into:

- **superficial burns** when only the outer layers of the skin are damaged. The skin is red and it may swell and blister. Pain is severe.

- **deep burns** when the outer layers of the skin are destroyed. The skin may be charred, and there may be other areas of superficial burn.

Pain in the area of a deep burn may not be so severe because nerve endings have been destroyed but there is greater danger of infection because the skin is broken.

Shock is present in all burns, but the degree of shock increases with the size of the burned area. This is the result of the amount of fluid lost in the tissues and the intensity of the pain. Even a superficial burn of a large area of the body can cause severe shock.

FIRST AID

The aims of first aid for burns are to eliminate the cause, to keep tissue damage to a minimum, to reduce pain, swelling and blistering and to prevent contamination of the burned area:

- remove the casualty from the source of heat. Immediately reduce the temperature in the burned area by immersing the injured part in cold water or by applying towels soaked in cold water until the pain is reduced. Heat in burned tissue continues to spread and can cause more injury after the burning agent has been removed. To prevent further tissue damage, cool down the whole area as quickly as possible. Seconds count!

- remove constrictive clothing and jewellery (rings, bracelets, shoes, etc.) before swelling begins.

- remove dry corrosive chemicals by first brushing off any powder. Then flush the area with continuously running water for ten to fifteen minutes to flush away any remaining chemical. Flush liquid chemical off the skin immediately with running water. Remove contaminated clothing while continuing to flush the area. Chemicals in the eyes should be flushed out with gently flowing tepid water (*see chap. 9 - Eye Injuries*).

- in electric burns, shut off the electric current or remove live wires from the casualty (*see chap. 1 - Principles and Practices of Safety Oriented First Aid*) before starting first aid. Assess breathing and give artificial respiration if needed (*see chap. 3 - Artificial Respiration and CPR*). Dress wounds at the entry and exit sites and check for other injuries that may have been caused by the shock.

- cover the burned area lightly with a sterile dressing, a clean towel or a sheet if the area is large. Protect blisters so that they do not break.

- give first aid to slow the progress of shock (*see chap. 7 - Shock*).

- arrange for immediate medical aid.

If clothing must be removed because of chemical contamination or to expose the burned area, cut the clothing and remove it gently. Do not pull at pieces of cloth that are stuck to a burn.

PRECAUTIONS

When giving first aid for a serious burn:

- do not break blisters.

- do not breathe on, cough over or touch the burned area to prevent contamination.

- do not apply lotions, ointments, oils or butter to a burn that will need medical care. Remember, anything you apply will have to be removed at the hospital.

- do not cover a burn with cotton wool or other fluffy material.

Sips of water may be given if the casualty is conscious and complains of thirst.

Medical aid is needed for superficial burns that cover a large area, for all deep burns and for electric and chemical burns. Infants and the elderly should receive medical aid for even small burns, particularly if the burns are to the face, hands or genitals. These burns can result in respiratory problems or serious infections.

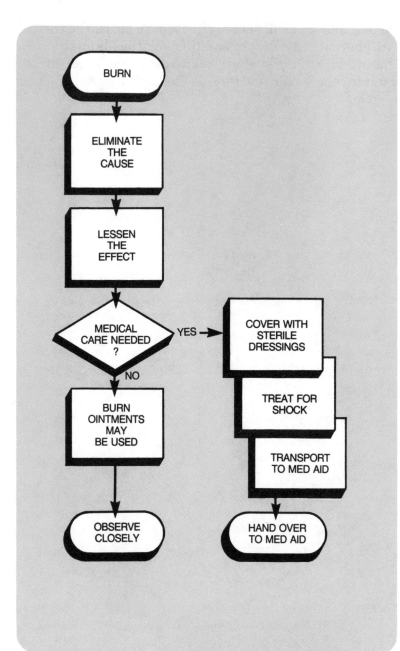

Fig. 10-1. Care of burns.

Small burns that will not require medical aid can be treated with pharmaceutically prepared burn ointments and creams. This includes minor sunburn, which can be immersed in cold water to relieve pain and then treated with a soothing lotion or cream.

11

ENVIRONMENTAL ILLNESSES AND INJURIES

HEAT AND COLD

The human body can adjust to a wide range of temperature if the person is fit, uses appropriate environmental protection and becomes gradually acclimatized. However, if someone is exposed suddenly without the proper protection to temperatures much hotter or colder than those in the normal environment, serious illnesses and injuries can result. Most of these illnesses and injuries can be prevented or their effects kept to a minimum by proper body conditioning and environmental protection and by recognizing the early signs. Prompt first aid reduces the lasting effects of exposure.

HEAT ILLNESSES

Illnesses from exposure to a hot environment are caused by the stresses placed on the body as it tries to maintain a normal temperature of 37.0°C *(98.6°F)*, or by the body's inability to maintain temperature control. Excessive sweating to cool the body causes a loss of body fluids and salts, resulting in **heat cramps**. Long exposure to hot, humid conditions decreases blood flow to the brain and to other vital organs, causing **heat exhaustion**. Vigorous exercise or hard labour in a hot environment with poor ventilation affects the body's mechanism for temperature control and can result in **heatstroke**.

PREVENTION

Try to moderate physical activity and to arrange for a gradual exposure to a hot environment. Protect the head from direct sunshine, and drink sufficient water to replace fluid loss from sweating. Prevent heat cramps by drinking water to which a small amount of salt has been added. A mixture of 5 millilitres *(mL)* of table salt *(1 full teaspoon)* to 1 litre *(a quart)* of water will make a 0.5% salt solution recommended for this purpose. Early recognition and first aid for heat illnesses prevents the development of more serious conditions and could save a life.

HEAT CRAMPS

SIGNS AND SYMPTOMS

Heat cramps can be recognized by painful muscle spasms in the arms, legs and abdomen and by excessive sweating. This condition is not serious and usually responds well to first aid.

FIRST AID

The aims of first aid are to replace body fluids and to relieve muscle spasms:

- place the casualty at rest in a cool place.

- give 250 mL *(an 8 oz. glass)* of slightly salted water *(0.5% salt solution)* to drink.

- give one more glass of salted water in 10 minutes time, if cramps persist, but do not give any more. There may be a more serious condition that needs medical attention.

- transport to medical aid if muscle spasms are not relieved.

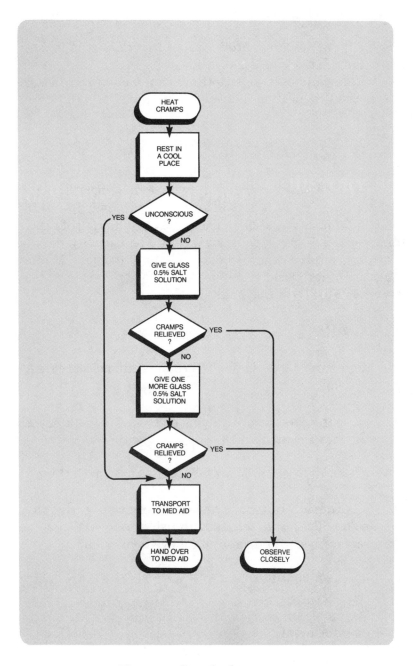

Fig. 11-1. Care for heat cramps.

HEAT EXHAUSTION

Heat exhaustion*(also called heat prostration)* is more serious than heat cramps. Excessive sweating causes a loss of body fluids and excessive clothing or the environment prevents the evaporation of sweat. The casualty will be in a state of shock.

SIGNS AND SYMPTOMS

Body temperature may range from just above normal to just below normal. The pulse will be weak and rapid. Breathing will be rapid and shallow. There may be blurring of vision, dizziness and loss of consciousness. The casualty may be sweating, but the skin will be cold, clammy and pale. He may have painful muscle spasms, as in heat cramps, and may become nauseated and vomit.

FIRST AID

First aid for heat exhaustion is a combination of the care for heat cramps and for shock:

• place the person at rest, lying down in a cool place, with the feet elevated;

• loosen tight clothing and remove excessive clothing;

• give the fully conscious casualty as much slightly salted water *(0.5% salt solution)* to drink as he will take to replace body fluids and to relieve heat cramps;

• if unconsciousness occurs, place the casualty in the recovery position;

• monitor breathing closely;

• transport to medical aid.

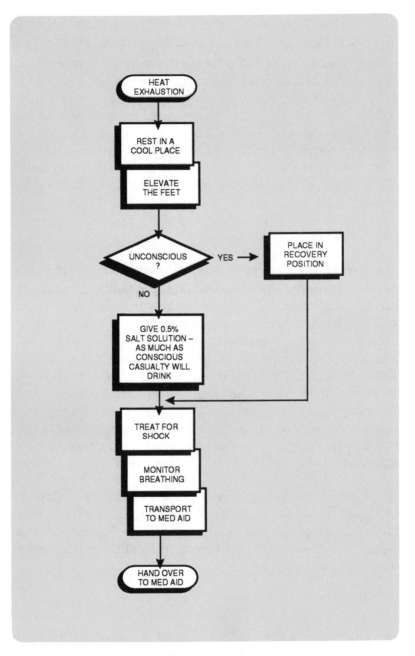

Fig. 11-2. Care for heat exhaustion.

HEATSTROKE

Prolonged exposure in a hot, humid, poorly ventilated environment puts excessive stress on the body as it attempts to cool itself. ***Classic heatstroke*** occurs when the body's temperature control mechanism fails; sweating ceases and body temperature rises rapidly. ***Exertional heatstroke*** occurs as a result of heavy physical exertion in high temperatures; sweating continues but again, body temperature rises rapidly. Heatstroke can result in permanent damage or death if first aid is not given immediately. Medical aid is needed urgently.

SIGNS AND SYMPTOMS

Body temperature will rise, reaching 42°C to 44°C *(108°F to 111°F)*. Initially, the pulse will be rapid and full, but it will become weak in later stages. Breathing may be noisy. There will be changes in the state of consciousness, progressing from headache and dizziness to total loss of consciousness and coma. There may be convulsions, nausea and vomiting. The face is usually flushed and hot and the skin dry. In exertional heatstroke, the skin will be sweaty.

Learn to recognize the difference between heat exhaustion and heatstroke by the casualty's body temperature and the appearance of the skin. In heat exhaustion, body temperature ranges from just above normal to below normal; in heatstroke, temperature rises rapidly, reaching 42°C to 44°C *(108°F to 111°F)*. In heat exhaustion, the skin is pale, cold and clammy; in heatstroke, the skin is flushed, hot and either dry or wet. Heatstroke can be fatal if body temperature is not reduced quickly.

FIRST AID

The most urgent first aid for heatstroke is to reduce body temperature as quickly as possible to near the normal value

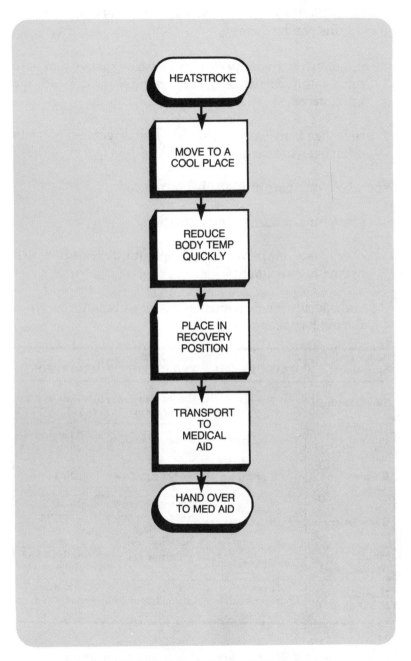

Fig. 11-3. Care for heatstroke.

of 37.0°C *(98.6°F)*. The casualty's life depends on how quickly this can be done:

- immerse the casualty in a cold bath or sponge him with cold water, particularly the armpits, neck, head and groin areas;

- cover the body with wet sheets, and direct cool air with a fan over the casualty if a cold bath is not available.

When body temperature has been reduced:

- place him in the recovery position;

- check body temperature at frequent intervals in case it begins to rise again;

- transport to medical aid in a car or ambulance in which the air has been cooled.

Signs and Symptoms	HEAT CRAMPS	HEAT EXHAUSTION	HEATSTROKE
Temperature	Normal	May be above or below normal	Elevated - as high as 44°C (111°F)
Pulse	Weak and regular	Weak and rapid	Rapid and full - becoming weaker
Respiration	Normal	Rapid and shallow	Noisy
Consciousness	Fully conscious	Headache, blurred vision, dizziness and loss of consciousness	Headache, dizziness, restlessness, coma
Skin Appearance	Excessive sweating	Pale, cold and clammy	Flushed, hot and either dry or wet
Muscular Reaction	Spasms of extremities and abdomen	Spasms of extremities and abdomen	Convulsions, nausea and vomiting

Fig. 11-4. Heat illnesses — signs and symptoms.

COLD INJURIES

Exposure to cold can cause generalized cooling, and can reduce the body's temperature to dangerous levels. When the temperature inside the trunk *(core temperature)* drops below normal, the condition is called **hypothermia**. Cold can also damage surface tissues, causing such injuries as **frostbite** and **immersion foot**.

PREVENTION

Prevention of cold injuries begins with understanding the conditions in the environment that cause these injuries. The speed of the wind, combined with the temperature of the air, produces a **wind-chill factor** that determines how quickly exposed skin will freeze. A still-air temperature of minus 10°C *(+14°F)* poses no great threat, but when this is combined with a wind force of 48 km/h, the chilling effect is minus 33°C *(-27.4°F)* !

The degree of wind and weather protection provided by outer clothing, the age and physical condition of the individual and the level of nourishment determine how long the individual can be exposed safely to a cold environment. Observe these safety tips to avoid cold injuries:

- **stay warm** — wear clothing that retains body heat without causing sweating. Several layers of loose-fitting clothing have a greater protective value than one thick item of constrictive clothing. Keep the head covered to prevent heat loss.

- **stay dry** — avoid getting wet, even from sweating. Any moisture on the skin increases loss of body heat by evaporation, and wet clothing has little insulating value.

- **stay safe** — limit the time spent in the cold and stay with a partner so that you can check each other for signs of frostbite and hypothermia. This is called the "buddy system."

- **eat well** — eat raisins, nuts and other easily converted high energy foods at regular intervals.

Avoid fatigue and the use of tobacco and alcohol. These contribute to heat loss and increase the chances of cold injury.

FIRST AID
GENERAL RULES

Give first aid for cold injuries as follows:

- shelter the person from the cold as much as possible;

- remove wet clothing gently, and replace with dry warm clothing;

- loosen tight clothing, boots and gloves and remove rings from injured hands before swelling of the fingers occurs;

- provide warmth with a campfire or heat from your body; place your hand over a frostbitten area;

- give warm, sweet drinks if the casualty is conscious;

- handle the injured parts gently to prevent further damage;

- if you must thaw a frozen part, use warm water baths at a temperature of 40°C *(104 F)*; warmer water will cause extreme pain;

- if blistered areas must be bandaged, place the dressings and bandages lightly over the injury to prevent breaking the blisters;

- obtain medical aid as soon as possible.

Take the following precautions in the care of cold injuries:

- **do not thaw** a frozen limb unless the casualty can remain warm and medical aid is not readily available;

- **do not thaw** a frozen foot if the casualty has to walk on it;

- **do not apply snow or cold water** to the frozen areas;

- **do not rub frozen areas**, because frozen tissues contain ice crystals that can cut and destroy tissue cells;

- **do not make the casualty move** any more than is absolutely necessary.

HYPOTHERMIA

Hypothermia is defined as a low body temperature. In first aid, the condition of hypothermia is said to exist when the body's core temperature drops to a level of 35.0°C *(95.0°F)* or lower.

SIGNS AND SYMPTOMS	PROGRESSIVE STAGES OF HYPOTHERMIA		
	MILD	MODERATE	SEVERE
Body core temperature	35°C to 32°C	32°C to 27°C	below 27°C
Pulse	normal range	slow and weak	weak, irregular or absent
Respirations	normal range	slow and shallow	slow or absent
Appearance and behaviour	shivering, slurred speech	stumbling, violent shivering	shivering stops
State of consciousness	conscious, but withdrawn	sleepy, confused, irrational	unconsciousness

Fig. 11-5. Signs and symptoms of hypothermia.

Hypothermia usually results from immersion in cold water or long exposure to cold air. Those most susceptible to hypothermia are the very young, the elderly, persons who are ill or those under the influence of alcohol or drugs. Hypothermia is a condition that becomes more severe in progressive stages. You can usually recognize each stage by the casualty's signs and symptoms as listed in the table above.

FIRST AID

Follow the general rules of first aid for cold injuries and in particular:

- handle the casualty gently and carefully with as little movement as possible. Rough handling of a casualty in a state of hypothermia can cause a serious disturbance of heart rhythm.

- remove wet clothing gently, and place the person in a warm area, such as a warmed sleeping bag.

- apply a rescuer's body heat to the areas where heat loss is the greatest — the head, neck, chest, armpits and groin.

- monitor breathing and circulation carefully, and give direct artificial respiration or CPR for hypothermic casualties whose breathing has stopped or who are in cardiac arrest.

- do not delay getting the casualty to medical aid, but do so very gently.

Severe hypothermia *(shivering has stopped)* may result in unconsciousness, stopped breathing and a very slow, weak or absent pulse. If breathing stops, mouth-to-mouth artificial respiration should be started immediately. Check the carotid pulse carefully *(for up to 2 minutes)* to ensure that even a slow, weak pulse will be detected. ***CPR must not be started if there is any sign of a pulse, no matter how slow or weak.***

If a pulse cannot be felt, the CPR trained rescuers must decide whether or not to begin chest compressions. Bearing in mind that they must be prepared to maintain CPR until medical aid is reached, the following factors should be considered:

1. Are the rescuers physically able to carry out CPR for the time required to reach medical aid?

2. Are the rescuers themselves in a mild state of hypo-thermia or at risk of hypothermia?

3. Is the estimated time until medical aid is reached so long *(more than an hour)* that CPR cannot reasonably be maintained?

If the answer to any of these questions indicates that CPR cannot be maintained until the casualty is in medical hands, the procedure should not be started.

SUPERFICIAL FROSTBITE

Frostbite of the ears, face, fingers or toes is most often superficial and can be recognized by the white appearance of the skin. The area may be numb, but firm to the touch.

Gradually rewarm superficial frostbite with the steady pressure and warmth of the hands. Breathing on the frostbitten area or placing the injured part in close contact with a warm area of your own body such as the armpit, may be all that is needed to restore circulation to the area.

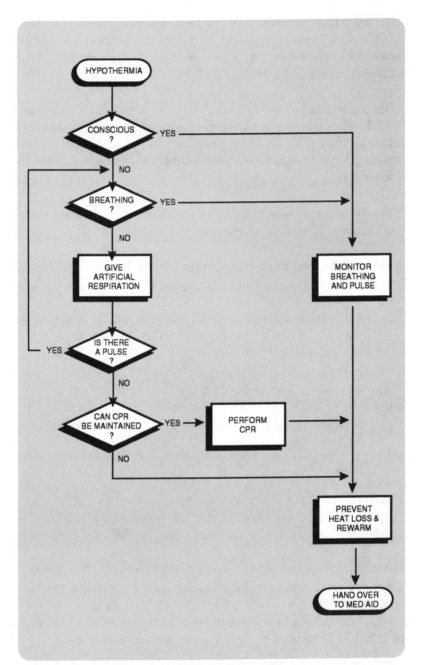

Fig. 11-6. Care for hypothermia.

DEEP FROSTBITE

As frostbite progresses, the frozen part becomes white, waxy and numb. It feels cold and hard to the touch. This frostbite is deep and medical aid is needed. Transport the casualty by stretcher, particularly if lower limbs are frozen. If the casualty must walk to get help, do not thaw the frozen limb. Walking on a frozen foot will not cause serious additional damage provided it has not been thawed. Help the casualty with the pick-a-back carry or the human crutch *(see chap. 14 - Rescue and Transportation)* to reduce contact with rough ground.

IMMERSION FOOT

Wet cooling of the feet for prolonged periods causes immersion foot. In the initial stages, the feet are cold, swollen and waxy and may be numb. After rewarming, they become red, swollen and hot, and blisters may develop. In advanced stages, gangrene may develop. Immersion foot can be prevented by keeping the feet dry. Carry spare socks in a warm, dry place, such as the inside pocket of your jacket, and change them often. Place damp socks inside your jacket to dry. If spare socks are not available, remove the wet socks, wring them as dry as possible and put them back on.

First aid consists of removing wet footwear as soon as possible, rewarming and gently drying the feet and preventing infection. Medical aid is needed.

12

POISON, BITES AND STINGS

POISONS

A poison is any substance that can cause illness or death when it is absorbed into the body. An antidote is a substance that acts against a poison to offset its effects.

PREVENTION

Most accidental poisonings can be prevented if the presence of poisons is recognized and proper care is taken in their use and storage. The average household has as many as 250 poisonous substances[1] used in medicines, in cleaning products, for plant care, or for hobbies and crafts. By law, all consumer products must be labelled to show their chemical content, precautions for use and storage, and specific first aid in case of accidental poisoning. Workplace Hazardous Materials Information System (WHMIS) regulations require that hazardous chemicals in the workplace be identified and that Material Safety Data Sheets (MSDS) describe the precautions in their use and the first aid to be given for accidental over-exposure *(see chap. 1 - Principles and Practices of Safety Oriented First Aid)*.

---

[1] *How To Poison-Proof Your Home.* Health and Welfare Canada, Ottawa, 1984.

To prevent accidental poisoning:

- keep household and drug products in their original containers for identification, so that instructions will be available each time they are used, and so that label information will be at hand in case of poisoning.

- read label instructions on containers before using, and follow the directions carefully. Read, understand and follow MSDS instructions for industrial chemicals.

- do not put harmful products in food or drink containers.

- destroy foods which you believe may be contaminated.

- flush unused portions of medicines down the toilet and dispose of empty containers.

- ventilate areas where toxic chemicals are used — open windows and doors so that fumes do not become concentrated.

- operate gas combustion engines where there is good ventilation, preferably outdoors.

- prevent medication errors by carefully checking the five *RIGHTS* for giving medicines — the *RIGHT MEDICINE*, the *RIGHT PERSON*, the *RIGHT DOSE*, the *RIGHT TIME*, the *RIGHT METHOD*.

- keep all harmful products out of the reach of children. Do not leave medications in a purse or on a night table where children can get at them.

- do not take medicines in front of children, because they may imitate you.

- when children need medicine, call it medicine and not candy.

- learn to identify poisonous plants, and warn children that plants may be poisonous.

- call the Poison Information Centre for prevention and first aid information in advance of going to an isolated area where you will be more than one hour away from a telephone.

HISTORY, SIGNS AND SYMPTOMS

You need as much information about a poisoning accident as possible so that the proper first aid can be started without delay. Act quickly but calmly.

History

Four basic facts you should know before giving first aid are:

- **what substance was taken**. Container labels should identify the poison. If not, save urine and vomitus for analysis.

- **how much poison was taken**. Make an estimate of the quantity that may have been taken based on the number of pills originally in the container or the amount of chemical in the bottle, and the number of pills or the amount of chemical remaining.

- **how was the poison taken**. First aid may differ for poisons taken by mouth, absorbed through the skin, injected into the blood or breathed into the lungs.

- **what is the elapsed time** since the poison was taken. The length of time the poison has been in the body will help to determine the first aid and medical care needed.

Signs and Symptoms

If the history does not reveal what poison was taken or by what means it was taken, the signs and symptoms may be helpful in determining how the poison was taken. Poisons that have been:

- **taken by mouth** usually cause nausea, abdominal cramps and vomiting. They may discolour the lips, cause burns in the mouth or leave an odour on the breath.

- **absorbed through the skin** frequently cause a reddening of the skin and may affect consciousness, breathing and pulse.

- **injected through the skin** usually irritate the point of entry and affect consciousness, breathing and pulse.

- **inhaled** may cause problems with breathing. They may affect consciousness and the pulse. Signs and symptoms may include coughing, chest pain and difficult breathing. Prolonged exposure to natural gas used for heating and carbon monoxide (CO) from combustion engines will cause a headache, dizziness, unconsciousness, stopped breathing and cardiac arrest.

FIRST AID FOR POISONING
GENERAL RULES

If the casualty is unconscious or becomes unconscious, do not waste time. Place the casualty in the recovery position and monitor breathing closely. Gather any available information on the suspected poison and transport the casualty to medical aid urgently.

If the casualty is conscious call the Poison Information Centre *(see the front pages of your telephone directory)* or a doctor, give whatever information you have and follow their advice on treatment. If there is no centre in your area, call the Ottawa centre anytime at 1-800-267-6351. If a Poison Information Centre or a doctor cannot be reached quickly, give first aid to eliminate the poison or reduce its effects, however, do not delay getting the casualty to medical aid.

Eliminate the Poison and Reduce its Effects

Poisons that have been taken by mouth should not be diluted. If the casualty is conscious, wipe any poisonous or corrosive residue from the casualty's face and rinse or wipe out the mouth. Never induce vomiting except on the advice of the Poison Information Centre or the doctor; many poisons will cause more damage when vomited.

If you are advised to do so, vomiting can be induced by giving **ipecac syrup.** Sealed, one-dose bottles (14 mL) of ipecac syrup are available at most pharmacies. At least two bottles should be kept in the home, out of reach of children, for emergency use. Use ipecac only on the advice of a Poison Information Centre or a doctor. You will be instructed to give a quantity of clear fluids to drink — water or juices (not milk) — following the administration of the ipecac syrup. Milk prevents the emetic action of the ipecac and it should not be given to the casualty.

If you do not have ipecac, the Poison Information Centre may instruct you to induce vomiting by giving the conscious casualty 30 to 45 mL (2-3 tablespoons) of liquid dish detergent in 250 mL (8 oz.) of water to drink. Vomiting caused by gagging is usually ineffective. Never use salt or mustard to induce vomiting.

Poisons absorbed through the skin should be washed off, first with large amounts of clear running water and then

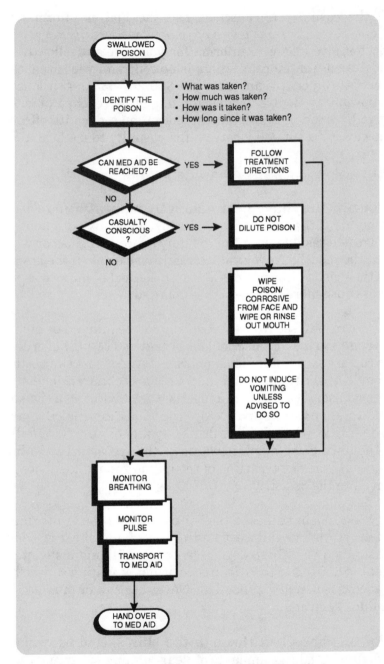

Fig. 12-1. First aid for poisons taken by mouth.

with soap and water. Pay careful attention to hidden areas such as under the fingernails and in the hair.

Injected poisons. Flush the skin at the point of entry of injected poisons. Try to delay the circulation of the poison throughout the body by placing the casualty at rest and keeping the affected limb at heart level.

Inhaled poisons. Remove the person from the source of the gas or vapor to fresh air to eliminate as much of the poison as possible from the lungs. If breathing has stopped, give artificial respiration *(see chap. 3 - Artificial Respiration).*

Monitor breathing closely and give mouth-to-mouth artificial respiration if this is needed. If the first aider could be affected by the poison, an alternative method of artificial respiration should be used. Monitor circulation and, when necessary, give CPR if you are trained in these techniques. Watch for vomiting. If it occurs, keep the unconscious person in the recovery position. Prevent the casualty from injuring himself if he goes into convulsions. Give first aid for shock *(see chap. 7 - Shock).*

Medical Aid

Transport the unconscious casualty to medical aid immediately. The conscious casualty should be transported to medical aid as soon as initial first aid is given.

ANIMAL BITES

Animal bites cause puncture wounds that carry contaminated saliva into the body. Domestic animal bites are dangerous, usually because of infection. Bites from wild animals, such as bats, foxes, skunks and raccoons, are more likely to carry the rabies virus and may be fatal if the casualty is not treated and immunized quickly. Bats are of particular concern, and any bite from a bat should be considered to be infected with the rabies virus.

FIRST AID

All animal bites that penetrate the skin should be seen by a doctor. If there is the least suspicion of rabies, medical aid is needed urgently.

While waiting for transportation to medical aid, give first aid as follows:

- allow the wound to bleed. Some bleeding helps to cleanse the wound. Control bleeding if it is severe.

- wash the wound with antiseptic soap or detergent.

- rinse with running water as hot as the person can bear, or apply a salt solution.

- apply a dressing and bandage, and transport to medical aid.

RABIES

Rabies should be suspected in domestic animals if they behave in an unusual way *(the gentle dog or cat that attacks for no apparent reason and shows fear of its owner)* and in all attacks by wild animals. The rabies virus can be transmitted to anyone who handles the diseased animal or who touches the area of the wound that carries the virus.

Be especially careful in giving first aid to anyone you suspect may have been exposed to rabies and in handling the live or dead animal involved. Scrub your hands thoroughly after contact to reduce the risk of infection.

If the animal can be captured without risk, it should be kept for examination. If the animal must be killed, try to keep the head intact so that the brain can be examined for the presence of rabies.

Even if a person has been exposed to a rabid animal, rabies can be prevented if immunization against the disease is given quickly. Immunization now consists of five inoculations given in the muscle of the arm or leg and is no more painful than a pinprick. This new method of immunization is much less painful than the previous method and there are fewer complications.

SNAKEBITE

The rattlesnake is the only poisonous snake found in the wild in Canada. Varieties of this snake are found in parts of British Columbia, Alberta, Saskatchewan and Ontario. They are not numerous, and snakebites are not common. A rattlesnake bite leaves two puncture holes in the skin, and a burning sensation is felt in the area. This is followed by swelling and discolouration, severe pain, weakness, sweating, nausea, vomiting and chills. Breathing may be affected.

FIRST AID

A rattlesnake bite needs first aid urgently. Ensure that you and the casualty are not in danger of a second bite; move the casualty to safety as there may be other snakes in the area. Give first aid to prevent the venom from circulating throughout the body:

- reassure the casualty;

- place him at rest, and keep him quiet to reduce circulation;

- flush the bite with soapy water, but do not apply cold compresses or ice;

- apply a constricting band *(see below – Constriction for Bites and Stings);*

- immobilize the limb and keep it at heart level;

- transport to medical aid as quickly as possible.

Precautions

Do not let a snakebite casualty walk if there is any other method of transportation to medical aid. Do not give alcoholic beverages to drink.

Do not attempt to suck poison out of the punctures with your mouth. Venom can pass through the thin tissues of your mouth and be absorbed into your blood. You would then become the second casualty.

CONSTRICTION FOR BITES AND STINGS

When a serious bite or sting occurs on a limb, a constricting band should be placed on the limb between the bite and the heart to slow the spread of the poison through the casualty's body. The recommended material for a constricting band is soft rubber tubing, however, a narrow triangular bandage or an elastic bandage may be used.

Place the constricting band 5 to 10 cm *(2 to 4 inches)* above the wound. **Do not tie the band too tight.** You should be able to slip two fingers under the band. If you see signs of loss of circulation below the band, the band must be loosened. Swelling will occur with this type of injury; therefore, you must adjust the constricting band so it does not become too tight. Constricting bands should not be placed around a joint, or around the head, neck or trunk.

INSECT BITES AND STINGS

In most persons, an insect bite or sting causes only a painful swelling with redness and itching. Bee and wasp stings, however, may cause a severe allergic reaction in some people. Look for hives, swelling around the eyes and mouth, nausea and vomiting, and breathing difficulties. When these signs occur, obtain medical aid urgently.

FIRST AID

Do not delay transporting the casualty to medical aid. If time permits, give first aid as follows:

- ask the person if they have medication which they take for such a reaction and help them to take prescribed medication if it is available.

- if the insect bite or sting is on a limb, place a constricting band above the bite site and keep the limb at heart level. Place the casualty in the recovery position or any position that makes breathing easier.

Provide first aid to the site of a bite or sting as follows:

- apply rubbing alcohol, a weak ammonia solution or a paste of bicarbonate of soda *(baking soda)* and water. Alcohol and ammonia should not be used near the eyes.

- when the stinger remains in the skin, remove it by carefully scraping it and its attached poison sac from the skin. Do not use tweezers or anything that may squeeze more poison into the body.

- if the sting is in the mouth, give the person a mouthwash of one teaspoonful of bicarbonate of soda to a glass of water or give him a piece of ice to suck. If there is swelling in the mouth, or if there is difficulty breathing, monitor the person closely. Get medical aid.

OTHER BITES

Leeches are found in swamps, ponds, lakes and stagnant water. Some feed on the warm blood of animals or humans. They make a tiny lesion in the skin and once a leech has attached itself, attempts to remove it by force may not be successful and may increase the risk of infection.

First aid for lesions from leeches consists of:

- removing the leech by applying salt, a heated pin, a lighted match, turpentine or oil to its body. This will cause the leech to detach itself from the skin and to fall off intact. Do not pull or scrape them off the skin.

- cleansing the area and relieving irritation with a weak ammonia solution or a paste of baking soda and water.

Ticks are found in abundance throughout the forests in some parts of Canada. They drop from the foliage onto animals and humans, biting through the skin and anchoring themselves to the tissue with barbed mouth parts. Infection from the tick may be harmful and the tick should be removed. If one tick is found, check for others on the body and clothing.

First aid for bites from ticks consists of:

- removing the embedded tick by grasping it as close to the casualty's skin as possible and pulling away from the skin with an even, steady pull. It is preferable to use tweezers for this manoeuvre. If fingers must be used, they should be covered with gloves or tissue paper. Keep the dislodged tick for later identification.

- cleansing the area around the bite to prevent infection. Following this, wash your hands.

- seeking medical aid because of the risk of disease transmission by the tick. The dislodged tick should be given to medical personnel for identification.

13

MEDICAL CONDITIONS

HEART DISEASE, STROKE, DIABETES, EPILEPSY AND CONVULSIONS

Many medical disorders and diseases result in emergencies that need urgent care. A basic knowledge of the disease, its signs and symptoms, and the first aid required may mean the difference between a slow or quick recovery and could save a life.

HEART DISEASES

Heart diseases are those conditions that interfere with the normal functions of the heart. The most common heart diseases can cause angina, heart attack and heart failure. Heart diseases are a major cause of death and are linked in some ways to the way we live. Certain conditions, such as high blood pressure, high levels of blood cholesterol, stress, smoking, lack of proper exercise, diet and excessive weight, are known to be related to the incidence of heart disease.

Adopt a healthy lifestyle:

- have blood pressure checks taken at regular intervals.

- avoid stress. Recognize stressful situations, and learn to cope with these in a non-stressful way.

- do not smoke.

- exercise regularly and in moderation. See your doctor if there is the slightest suspicion of a heart problem.

- control body weight and blood cholesterol with a diet recommended by a medical professional.

HEART ATTACK

The condition which most often results in a cardiac emergency is a heart attack. A heart attack occurs when blood supply to a part of the heart muscle is partially or completely blocked. The lack of oxygen to the tissues causes a part of the heart muscle to die (myo*cardial infarct)* and may disrupt or stop heart action. Early recognition of the onset of a heart attack and giving the appropriate first aid can often prevent cardiac arrest and death.

Learn to recognize the warning signs and symptoms of an impending heart attack. Remember that the casualty will often deny, even to himself, that he is having a heart attack.

Inform fellow workers if you have a heart problem. If symptoms develop while driving a motor vehicle, get off the road and stop the vehicle as quickly as possible.

Encourage family members and co-workers to take training in first aid, including cardiopulmonary resuscitation (CPR) and learn the quickest way to contact emergency medical services in your community. Display ambulance telephone numbers near the telephones at work and at home.

SIGNS AND SYMPTOMS

Any one or more of the following signs and symptoms indicate a possible heart attack:

- fear and apprehension;

- severe crushing chest pain and pain in the neck, shoulders, arms, throat, jaw, elbows and fingers *(angina)*;

- feeling of indigestion;

- shortness of breath;

- pallor, sweating, blue-grey colour around the lips, nail beds, ears and face and other signs of shock;

- nausea and vomiting;

- unconsciousness;

- absence of pulse.

FIRST AID

Give first aid for any suspected heart attack as follows:

- call for an ambulance or transport the person immediately to a medical facility;

- place the person at rest in a semisitting position;

- assist the conscious person to take any prescribed medication;

- loosen tight clothing at the neck, chest and waist;

- reassure the casualty to lessen fear and anxiety;

- keep the person warm to slow the progress of shock.

Monitor breathing and circulation closely. Assist with breathing and, if the heart stops, start CPR if you are trained in these techniques.

STROKE

Stroke is a condition in which a part of the brain ceases to function because its blood supply is disrupted, cutting off the oxygen supply to the brain cells. Severe stroke can cause death; a less severe case can be recognized by its signs and symptoms.

SIGNS AND SYMPTOMS

A stroke may occur at any age, but usually occurs in middle-aged or elderly people and is often associated with high blood pressure. A sudden change in such a person may indicate a stroke, and you should look for the following:

- changes in level of consciousness *(see chap.6 - Unconsciousness);*

Fig. 13-1. Unequal size of pupils may indicate a stroke or head injury.

- unequal size of the pupils of the eyes;

- paralysis of the muscles of the face with difficulty in speaking and swallowing;

- numbness or paralysis of the hands and feet, particularly on one side;

- mental confusion;

- loss of bladder and bowel control;

- convulsions.

FIRST AID

First aid for a stroke casualty is limited to calling for an ambulance and protecting the person until help arrives. While awaiting medical aid:

- make the person comfortable, semisitting if conscious.

- if the person becomes unconscious, place him in the recovery position on the paralyzed side to make breathing easier.

- loosen tight clothing.

- give nothing by mouth if the person is unconscious. If the conscious person wants a drink, moisten the lips and tongue with a wet cloth.

- reassure and avoid excitement.

Do not use heating pads or hot water bottles on a stroke casualty. Because they are unable to feel the heat and tell you if it is too hot, burns may result.

DIABETES

Diabetes, in a simplified definition, is a condition in which the body is unable to convert its sugar intake into energy, because of a lack of **insulin.** Insulin is normally produced by the body in sufficient quantities to maintain a proper insulin and sugar balance. If the body does not produce enough insulin, it develops a sugar imbalance and the person is said to be a diabetic. A diabetic must control his diet and may have to take artificial insulin or other anti-diabetic medication to balance sugar with insulin levels.

A **diabetic emergency** will occur when there is a severe imbalance between the amount of insulin in the body and the sugar level in the blood. This usually occurs because of improper diet, or too much artificial insulin. Diabetic emergencies are known as **diabetic coma,** and **insulin shock.** Anti-diabetic medication, if taken incorrectly, can cause a severe drop in blood sugar *(a condition called hypoglycemia)* and produces signs and symptoms that resemble insulin shock.

HISTORY, SIGNS AND SYMPTOMS

The signs and symptoms of diabetic coma and insulin shock, as listed in the following table, are difficult to interpret, but it is not important that the First Aider be able to do so. Try to confirm, by questioning the casualty or checking for a medic alert device on his wrist or on a neck pendant, that the person is a diabetic. Ask the conscious casualty about his medication and what he needs.

Signs & Symptoms	INSULIN SHOCK *(needs sugar)*	DIABETIC COMA *(needs insulin)*
Pulse	Full, rapid	Weak, rapid
Respirations	Shallow	Deep, sighing
State of Consciousness	Faintness to unconsciousness developing quickly	Gradual onset of unconsciousnes
Skin	Pale, sweating	Flushed, dry
Breath Odour	Odourless	Musty apple or nail polish(acetone) odour
Behavioural Signs	Headache, trembling, confused, aggressive	Coma

Fig. 13-2. Diabetic emergencies — signs and symptoms.

FIRST AID

The aim of first aid for a diabetic emergency is to keep the casualty's condition from becoming worse until medical aid is obtained. If the conscious casualty explains what he needs, help him to take his medication or to find a sweet substance to eat or drink. If there is doubt whether sugar or insulin is needed, give the conscious casualty a drink sweetened with 30 mL *(two tablespoons)* of sugar, or some other sweet substance. This will do no harm and could be beneficial.

If the casualty becomes unconscious, protect him from further injury *(see chap. 6 - Unconsciousness)* and get medical aid urgently.

EPILEPSY

Epilepsy is a disorder of the nervous system characterized by seizures which may involve partial or complete loss of consciousness and perhaps convulsions.

SIGNS AND SYMPTOMS

The signs will vary from a mild faint to a sudden loss of consciousness with convulsions, noisy breathing, grinding of the teeth, and frothy saliva around the mouth. Usually within minutes, the muscles gradually relax and the person will return to consciousness. He may have no recollection of the episode and may be dazed and confused.

FIRST AID

The aim of first aid is to protect the epileptic person from injury during the period of convulsions. Clear the area of curious onlookers, and give the casualty as much privacy as possible. Give first aid as follows:

- guide, but do not restrict movement;

- protect the person from injury;

- ensure an open airway and if possible put the person in the recovery position;

- do not insert anything between the teeth;

- maintain the person's privacy as much as possible; clear all nonessential persons away;

- do not leave the person unattended as a second seizure is quite possible. If a second seizure occurs within a few minutes, call for medical aid.

CONVULSIONS IN CHILDREN

Children with a high temperature may go into convulsions, which can be recognized by contractions of the muscles of the face and extremities. The body may become rigid and arch backward. The child may hold his breath, causing congestion and have froth at the mouth.

FIRST AID

The aim is to protect the child from injury and:

- gently attempt to maintain an open airway;

- loosen constrictive clothing;

- when convulsions cease, place the child in the recovery position;

- reassure the parents;

- obtain medical aid.

14

RESCUE AND TRANSPORTATION

Moving a person from an accident site poses dangers to the rescuer as well as to the casualty. The casualty's injuries may be made worse by movement and improper handling, and the rescuer can be injured by the improper use of rescue and transportation techniques. Therefore, always try to give necessary first aid where the casualty is found, and wait for the ambulance to move the person. In some circumstances, such as the following, it may be necessary or possible to move the casualty:

- there is danger from fire, water, gas or explosion;

- the need for hospital care is urgent, as in the case of a heart attack;

- necessary first aid cannot be given where the casualty is found;

- medical aid cannot come to the scene;

- the casualty's injuries can be protected during the move;

- the casualty's condition is not serious, and the move poses no danger.

If the person must be moved, select the method that will pose the least risk to the casualty and to yourself. Use as many bystanders as you need to keep risks to a minimum, and use proper techniques for lifting.

LIFTING TECHNIQUES
PROPER BODY MECHANICS

Avoid excessive pulling or twisting of the muscles of your back and legs when lifting a casualty or other heavy object:

* stand close to the object to be lifted;

* bend your knees; do not stoop;

* get a good grip on the object;

* lift together with other helpers, using the thigh, leg and abdominal muscles, but keep your back straight;

* when lowering heavy objects, reverse the procedure;

* when turning, follow the feet — do not twist your body.

Fig. 14-1. Lifting technique.

ONE-RESCUER CARRIES

One rescuer can move a casualty with the drag carry, the human crutch, the cradle carry or the pick-a-back carry, depending on the circumstances, the weight of the casualty and the strength of the rescuer.

DRAG CARRY

A drag carry, as the name implies, involves dragging the casualty while providing maximum protection to the head and neck. Because there is a real risk of aggravating the casualty's injuries, the drag carry should only be used in the most extreme cases when there is an immediate threat to life.

To use the drag carry for a casualty who is lying on his back:

* stand at the casualty's head facing his feet;

* crouch down so that you can ease your hands under the casualty's shoulders to grasp the clothing on each side;

Fig. 14-2. Drag carry.

* support the casualty's head between your forearms to prevent side-to-side turning (*rotation*) and dropping forward (*flexion*);

- move backward carefully and drag the casualty length-wise only as far as necessary for his safety.

If time permits, secure the casualty's hands together across his chest before dragging. If the casualty must be dragged down stairs, grasp him under the arms, support his head and neck on your chest, and descend the stairs backwards on your knees.

HUMAN CRUTCH

If one lower limb is injured, help the casualty to walk on his good leg while you give support to the injured side. Place the casualty's arm on the injured side around your neck and grasp the wrist firmly. Reach around the casualty's back with your free hand, and grasp his clothing at the waist. Instruct the casualty to step off with you on the inside foot. A walking stick, used on the uninjured side, will provide additional support.

Fig. 14-3. The human crutch.

CRADLE CARRY

Children and lightweight adults can be moved with a cradle carry if they are unable to walk. Kneel on one knee at the casualty's side. Place the casualty's near arm around your neck as you support his back and shoulders with your arm under his armpit. Pass the other arm under the knees to grasp the thighs. Ensure a good footing by placing your feet apart. Lift, using the muscles of the thighs and legs, while keeping the back straight and the abdominal muscles tense.

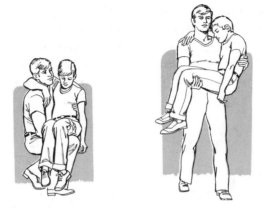

Fig. 14-4. Cradle carry from a kneeling position.

PICK-A-BACK CARRY

The pick-a-back carry can be used for a casualty who cannot walk, but who can use her upper limbs. If the casualty cannot help you to get herself into position, get her seated on a chair or table. Crouch with your back between the casualty's knees. Ensure that she has a firm grip around your neck. Pass both hands over the casualty's thighs and under her knees so that her thighs are cradled on your forearms. Keep your feet apart to ensure that you have a firm footing and lift, using the your leg and back muscles.

Fig. 14-5. The pick-a-back carry.

TWO-RESCUER CARRIES

Call on bystanders to assist in moving a casualty with carries
such as a four-hand seat, two-hand seat or the chair carry.
Remember that you are responsible for the casualty. You
must instruct the bystanders in what they are to do and
when they are to do it. Direct the lift to make it as safe and
as smooth as possible.

FOUR-HAND SEAT

A conscious casualty who has the use of her arms can be
carried on a four-hand seat formed by two rescuers. Each
rescuer grasps his own left wrist with his right hand then
grasps the right wrist of the other rescuer with his left hand
to form a square.

Fig. 14-6. The four-hand seat.

The casualty puts an arm around each rescuer's shoulders
and hoists up to allow the rescuers to pass their hands under

the buttocks and to position them under the thighs at a point of balance. Tell the casualty to hold on to maintain balance. Coordinate the lift by saying, "Prepare to lift. — Lift!" When the casualty is securely positioned, the bearers step off together, each using the inside foot.

TWO-HAND SEAT

A casualty, who is unable to support his upper body, can be carried by two rescuers, using the two-hand seat. The rescuers crouch on each side of a seated casualty and reach across his back to grasp his clothing at the waist on the opposite side. Each rescuer passes his other hand under the thighs, keeping his fingers bent and holding padding to protect against the fingernails when the hands are joined . The bent fingers of the two hands are hooked together to form a rigid seat. Direct the lift to ensure that each bearer steps off on the inside foot.

Fig. 14-7(a). Hand grip – two-hand seat.

Fig. 14-7(b). Hands in position– two-hand seat.

Fig. 14-7(c). The carry – two-hand seat.

CHAIR CARRY

A sturdy chair can be used to carry a conscious or an unconscious person through hallways and stairways. If the casualty is unconscious or helpless, strap her upper body and arms to the back of the chair. ***Do not use this carry for casualties with suspected neck or back injuries.***

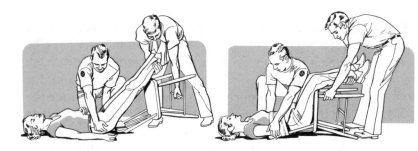

Fig. 14-8(a). Chair carry —
positioning the chair.

Fig. 14-8(b). Chair carry —
securing the casualty.

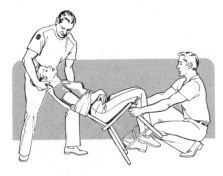
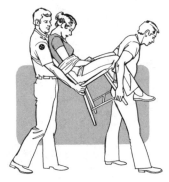

Fig. 14-8(c). Chair carry —
raising the chair.

Fig. 14-8(d). Chair carry.

If the casualty is lying on the ground, slide the back of the chair under the legs and buttocks and along the lower back. When the casualty is secure, raise the chair upright, while supporting the head and neck.

Two rescuers carry the chair, one at the front and one at the back. The rescuer at the back grasps the chair legs just under the seat while the one at the front crouches, his back between the casualty's legs, and grasps the front chair legs near the floor.

To descend stairs, the rescuer at the front turns to face the casualty. A third person acts as a guide and supports the front rescuer in the event of a loss of footing.

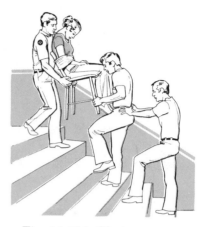

Fig. 14-8(e). Chair carry – descending stairs.

IMPROVISED STRETCHERS

When it is necessary to move a helpless casualty to medical aid or if the illness or injury allows only the most gentle movement, a stretcher should be used. A commercially prepared stretcher may not be available, but one can be improvised by using a tabletop, a door or two rigid poles and a blanket, clothing or grain sacks.

Test all improvised stretchers with someone equal to or heavier than the casualty to ensure that it will hold. This will not only reassure the casualty, it will prevent an accident that may cause further injury. Check the clearance of improvised stretchers to ensure that they will pass through hallways, doors and stairways without harm to the casualty. Non-rigid stretchers are not recommended for casualties with suspected neck and back injuries.

When making a non-rigid stretcher with poles, use two sticks of suitable length to hold the poles apart to the desired width of the stretcher. Tie these sticks securely to each pole at both ends of the stretcher.

IMPROVISED BLANKET STRETCHER

To make a non-rigid stretcher with two poles and a blanket, place the blanket flat on the ground, and place a pole one-third of the way from one end. Fold the one-third length of

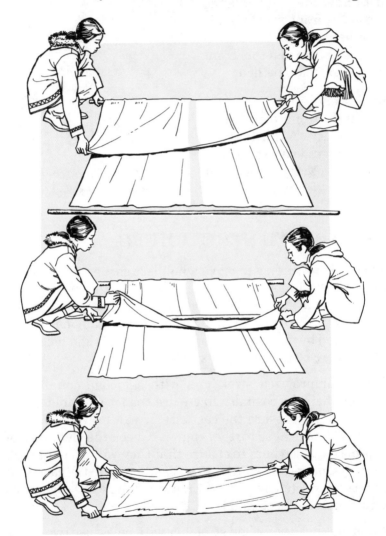

Fig. 14-9. The improvised blanket stretcher.

blanket over the pole, and place the second pole parallel to the first, about 15 cm *(6 inches)* from the folded end of the blanket. Fold the remaining blanket over the two poles.

IMPROVISED JACKET STRETCHER

A non-rigid stretcher can also be improvised from two jackets and two poles. Turn their sleeves inside out so that the sleeves are inside the body of the jacket Button, zipper or pin the jackets closed to make secure tubes. Lay the prepared jackets on the ground so that the top edge of one jacket meets the bottom edge of the other. Pass the poles through the sleeves of the two jackets, one on either side, to complete the stretcher. If the casualty is tall, prepare a third jacket as before and add it, top edge first, to the stretcher.

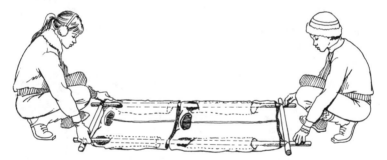

Fig. 14-10. Improvised jacket stretcher.

IMPROVISED SACK STRETCHER

Sacks and poles may also be used to make an improvised stretcher. Make small holes in the bottom corners of two grain or potato sacks. Place the sacks on the ground with their open ends touching. Pass the poles through the corner holes on either side to complete the stretcher. A third sack, open end first, may be added for taller casualties.

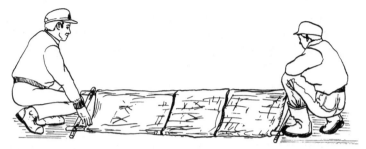

Fig. 14-11. Improvised sack stretcher.

PREPARING A STRETCHER

If there is only one blanket available to cover a casualty on a stretcher, you can provide the greatest amount of warmth by placing it on the stretcher so that diagonally opposite corners are at the head and foot. Place padding at appropriate places on the blanket to fill the natural hollows at the casualty's neck and back.

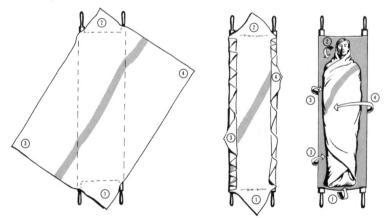

Fig. 14-12. Preparing a stretcher — one-blanket method.

Centre the casualty on the blanket, and cover the feet with the bottom corner (**1**). Bring the corner (**2**) at the head around the neck to the chest. Wrap the legs and lower body with one side **(3)**, and complete the procedure by bringing corner **(4)** over to tuck in on the opposite side.

If additional blankets are available, they can be placed under and over the casualty, but ensure that any wounds can be reached for observation during the journey.

BLANKET LIFT—FOUR BEARERS

Before attempting the blanket lift, test the blanket to ensure that it will carry the casualty's weight. Then, roll the blanket along its length for about half its width. Place the rolled edge along the casualty's injured side. Position bearers at the head and feet to maintain the head, neck and body in a line. Kneel at the casualty's shoulder and position another bearer at the waist to help in logrolling the casualty onto his uninjured side *(see chap. 8 - Injuries to Bones and Joints)*.

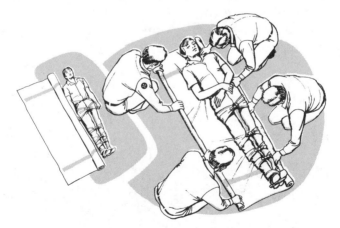

Fig. 14-13(a). Placing the casualty on a blanket.

The bearers at the head and feet act with you to ensure that the casualty's body is not twisted during the logroll. Move the blanket roll against the casualty's back, and turn him over toward the opposite side just enough so that the blanket can be unrolled toward you.

Roll the edges of the blanket up to each side of the casualty. Instruct the bearers to grip the roll at points along the body at the head and shoulders, and at the hip and lower legs. Keep the blanket taut as the casualty is lifted and placed on the stretcher. ***Do not use this lift if neck or back injuries are suspected.***

Fig. 14-13(b). The blanket lift with four bearers.

CARRYING THE STRETCHER

The stretcher can be carried by four or two bearers. You must direct the bearers and ensure that you are in a position that allows you to observe the casualty. If there are sufficient bearers to carry the stretcher, walk beside the stretcher and direct the bearers.

Fig. 14-14. Stretcher carry — four bearers.

To ensure the smoothest carry for the casualty, four bearers carrying a stretcher step off together on the foot nearest the stretcher and keep in step.

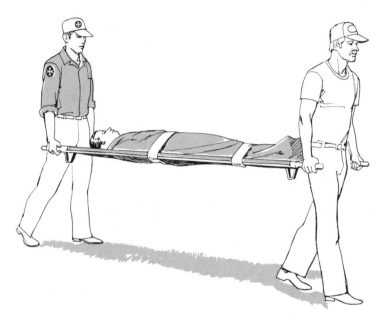

Fig. 14-15. Stretcher carry — two bearers.

Two bearers carrying a stretcher step off on opposite feet and walk out of step to provide a smoother carry for the casualty.

0393

00030390400000000000000000000000000000000000000

First Aid

We Can Help
An inexpensive course in first aid and safety awareness for children between the ages of 7 and 10. Ideal for integration with the junior school curriculum.

School Programme
Adapted from the Emergency and Standard First Aid courses, with lessons grouped into units to form a flexible time schedule suitable for any timetable requirements.

The Lifesaver
An introductory (2 ½ hour) first aid course for busy people. Students learn the essential first aid which may be required to save a life. Modules may be added to this course for special groups such as drivers or sports coaches.

Emergency First Aid Modular Course
A 6 ½ hour course comprised of 5 compulsory modules and 16 elective modules supported by audio-visual segments. This course, because of its flexibility, allows customization of course content to meet the first aid requirements of industry, business, government and schools.

Standard First Aid Modular Course
A 13 hour comprehensive programme comprised of 5 compulsory modules and 18 elective modules and supported by 16 audio-visual segments. CPR certification to the Heart Saver level is offered within the framework of this flexible programme. This course can be customized to meet the requirements of any person in industry, business, government or education.

Advanced First Aid - Level I
A one week (35 hour) programme that teaches the theory and practice of more advanced first aid procedures. This course is recommended for those who have specific first aid responsibilities.

Advanced First Aid - Level II
A two week (70 hour) comprehensive programme designed to train the Industrial First Aid Attendant.

National Instructor Training and Development Programme (NITDP)
One week (30 hour) course to develop and practice first aid and CPR teaching skills.

St. John Ambulance

St. John Ambulance Courses

CPR*

Level A (Heart Saver)
A 6 hour course that teaches one-rescuer CPR and choking manoeuvres for an adult casualty. This is the ideal CPR course for the lay person.

Level B (Heart Saver Plus)
An 8 hour course including Level A material and CPR and choking manoeuvres for an infant or a child casualty.

Level C (Basic Rescuer)
A 12 hour comprehensive course including one and two-rescuer CPR and choking manoeuvres for infant, child and adult casualties. This course is designed for those with specific health care responsibilities such as nurses and professional rescuers.

Level D (Child and Infant)
An 8 hour course designed for parents and day care providers which teaches CPR and choking manouevres for infant and child casualties.

Level E
Customized courses to provide CPR training to specific populations such as the physically challenged.

* All St. John Ambulance CPR courses are taught to the standards of the Heart and Stroke Foundation of Canada's Emergency Cardiac Care Committee.

Health Care

Family Health Care
A course designed to teach how to care for a sick or convalescent relative at home.

What Every Babysitter Should Know
A course on how to babysit infants, toddlers, and preschoolers. The emphasis is on safety, coping in emergency situations, and babysitting responsibilities.

Child Care in the Home
This course teaches the care of children from infancy to pre-school age, including information on common childhood ailments. This course is of particular interest to parents and day care providers.

Healthy Aging
A relaxed and informal health care course designed to provide older people with the skills to continue living healthy and productive lives.

Caring for the Aging
Teaches the basic nursing skills needed to look after an elderly person at home. This course is of interest to family members, homemakers, and other caregivers of the elderly.

National Health Care Instructor Training Programme
This course teaches the principles of learning and teaching as they apply to health care course instruction.

Serve your community in an important and unique way.

- 🕸 learn invaluable first aid and health care skills
- 🕸 apply your first aid skills to real life situations
- 🕸 help and care for others
- 🕸 meet new people
- 🕸 develop new and lasting friendships

Brigade members serve others in their community at almost every kind of event, from rock concerts to rodeos, and from conferences for the disabled to hockey and football games. You too can improve the quality of life in your community by making it a better and safer place to live. You'll be rewarded with the personal satisfaction of knowing that you've made a contribution. There's a place for you in the Brigade. Ask your instructor for details or call your local St. John Office today.

...Join the Brigade

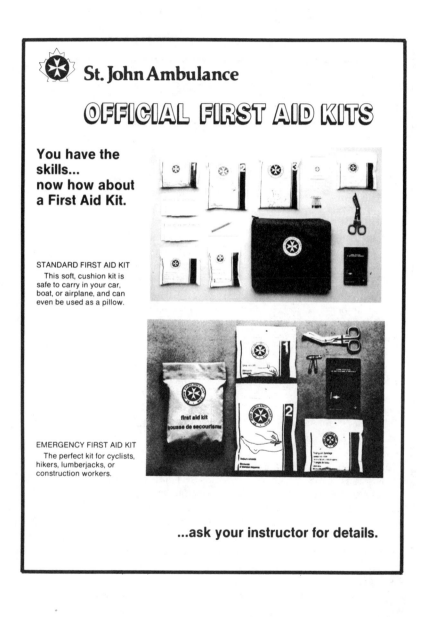

St. John Ambulance
Provincial Councils

Northwest Territories
P.O. Box 2640
Yellowknife, X1A 2P9
(403) 873-5658

British Columbia
6111 Cambie Street
Vancouver, V5Z 3B2
(604) 321-2651

Alberta
10975-124 Street
Edmonton, T5M 0H9
(403) 452-6565

Saskatchewan
2625-3rd Avenue
Regina, S4T 0C8
(306) 522-7226

Federal District
30 Driveway
Ottawa, K2P 1C9
(613) 236-3626

Quebec
405 de Maisonneuve Blvd. East
Montreal, H2L 4J5
(514) 842-4801

Manitoba
535 Doreen Street
Winnipeg, R3G 3H5
(204) 774-1851

Ontario
46 Wellesley Street East
Toronto, M4Y 1G5
(416) 923-8411

New Brunswick
P.O. Box 3599, Station"B"
Fredericton, E3A 5J8
(506) 458-9129

Nova Scotia
88 Slayter Street
Dartmouth, B3A 2A6
(902) 463-5646

Prince Edward Island
P.O. box 1235
Charlottetown, C1A 7M8
(902) 368-1235

Newfoundland
P.O. Box 5489
St. John's, A1C 5W4
(709) 726-4200

 St. John Ambulance